Extravagantly Loved

*21 Days of Powerful, Prophetic & Personal
Encounters with 'My First Love'*

By

Wendy Darline & Eric Ingram

Wendy Darline & Eric Ingram
Visit our website at www.theprodigalcouple.com

Printed in the United States of America

First Printing: June 1, 2018
100 Fold Life Publishing

ISBN-13 978-1-7324084-0-1
ISBN-10 1-7324084-0-8

DEDICATION...

To Our Loving Father, God
whose love endures forever

To Our Parents
for being our earthen examples of being divinely loved

To Our Children, James and Erica,
for enduring our flaws and teaching us the importance
of loving unconditionally

To Him Whom My Soul Loveth, My Beloved
By M Helen Ingram

Come, come winter for I must get to Spring
Where the cold rain has all but ceased and the humming birds do sing
To where the tender grapes appear and the orchards of pomegranate
And my Beloved is like a roe, and I the heart that panteth
Come you cold and desperately wicked of heart
That your lack in imagination be cast down
Your civility in its drossness, your darkness in its grossness
Must be stripped bare and plucked up from the ground
Stay with me you fail-safe flagons, you spirit filled water spouts
Winds blow upon my garden that my spice filled aromas may flow out
That my Beloved may eat of his pleasantness as He richly dwells within
Though I sleep, yet my heart rends me weak, as I wait for love's
embrace once again
My Beloved has made provision for me so why must I be denied
He was oppressed, afflicted, stricken, smitten, slaughtered, crucified
Though I weary, make me meek and lowly after the yearnings of my
Beloved's own heart Tempered together, pure and holy, as in
the Apothecary's Art
Have you seen Him whom my soul loveth
Before whom I am starkly naked and whom with everything I have to do
With the kiss of His mouth He declared me
Because of conception, I must pursue
Magnetize me to your divineness, I long to be drawn into your gates
Allow me to flourish in your lovely courts until dawn itself shall break
At last behind the veil of flesh where Love shall take its fill
Solacing ourselves with each caress, the Holy of Holies, the Will of wills
Come swift as a roe across the mountain let us take our fill of love til the
morning dawn Come, come winter for the love is everlasting,
and with loving kindness I AM drawn

Foreword

My God is a great god. The Lover of my wretched soul. Redeemer of my sinful life. Creator of my very being. I can truly say I did not know love until the love of God hunted me down, hogtied me, and held me hostage until this very day. At the time, I wasn't a practicing Christian. I wasn't praying--except before dinner. I wasn't going to church and I definitely wasn't reading the Bible. I was just living for myself, my newborn daughter, and the hopes of becoming a wildly successful screenwriter/actor.

All of that changed one hot summer night in August '08. I was a doorman/security at one of LA's swankiest celebrity nightclubs. On this particular night, it was about 2 am, closing time. As I was alerting all patrons it was time to go, a sweet lady grabbed my hand firmly, looked deep into my eyes, and said, "You don't belong here." I nodded politely, smiled and said, "Okay, but it's time to close up." She tightened her grip ever so slightly and said, "I'm serious. If you stay here, the people who you're supposed to help will perish." Perish? Really? "Okay, I got it," I said trying to pull away from her. She then said, "I haven't had a drink and I'm serious." I nodded in agreement knowing in my spirit there must be something to this, but no need to delve deeper into it at the moment. She finally left and I finished closing up with those words echoing in my spirit, "If you stay here, the people you're supposed to help will perish." Perish?? Who uses that word "perish"? One place is the Bible.

> *Prv 29:18: "Where there is no vision, the people perish: but he that keepeth the law, happy is he*

Another word for perish, *destroyed.*

Hosea 4:6: My people are destroyed for lack of knowledge.

My people perish/are destroyed from lack of knowledge and vision. Knowledge and vision of what? The knowledge of who God really is the vision Has for their lives. Our purpose is entwined with the vision God created for our lives. We need to seek Him in order to find out His vision and purpose for our lives. (This is exactly where I was at during this time in my life. I asked Him, "Lord, what it my purpose?" This lady's "perish" exhortation let me know loud and clear He heard my prayers... and He was coming for me.)

Later that same night, as I was walking to my car at around 3 am, I saw a book in the middle of Santa Monica Blvd. How odd is that? Curiously I went to pick it up. Its title: <u>Scriptures For The Purpose Driven Life</u>. Uh-oh, something was happening. I took the book home and left it on my desk for three days. Finally I said, "Okay, Lord, whatever you want to tell me, show me it on whatever page I turn to." I opened the book and the scripture facing me was *Jer 1:5:*

> *"Before I formed you in the womb I knew[a] you,*
> *before you were born I set you apart;*
> *I appointed you as a prophet to the nations."*

Whoa!, something's happening.

> *"And we know that all things work together for good to those who love God, to those who are the called according to His purpose. For whom He foreknew, He also predestined to be conformed to the image of His Son, that He might be the firstborn among many brethren. Moreover whom He predestined, these He also called; whom He*
> *called, these He also justified; and whom He justified, these He also glorified."*
> *Rom 8: 28-30 (NKJV)*

Who knew that the words that lady spoke back in 2008 was the start of my love affair with God, my first love? I was being courted. I was being called. I was already predestined according to Jer 1:5. Predestined for what? A prophet to the nations? Not little ol' me. I'm a comedian, an actor, a screenwriter; a prophet? Not. Or am I? According to his Word, I am who He says I am. Once I grabbed hold of that kingdom mentality, my life changed forever.

I love the everlasting God with a passion. Not just for miracles, signs and wonders He has shown me and done for me, but also for what He hasn't shown me nor done for me. Not just for the prayers He answered, but for the prayers He didn't answer. His love is unconditional; I am the apple of His eye *(Deut 32:10)*. The depth of His love is unthinkable, unreachable, unsearchable, and unattainable with our elementary human hearts and minds. It's so painfully profound; it leaves you speechless and sobbing uncontrollably in the fetal position. It forces you to ask the question, "Why me, Lord? What did I do to deserve this most precious gift from you?" The fact that He loved me so much he sent his only begotten son to die for me *(Jn 3:16)* while I was still living in sin *(Rom 5:8)* is just... It's unbelievably humbling.

And on that fate-filled morning when He told me Wendy is my wife that He chose for me. He chose me for her and her for me. There are roughly eight billion people on this planet and He chose me to be with one of His most precious daughters. That still sends chills up my spine. The day we met, I heard angels singing. I was like, "Am I being punked right now? Is anyone else hearing this?" He brought me Wendy. He brought me the love of my life. He brought me a warrior wife, a nurturing, sweet, hilariously funny, driven, loving, beautiful bride to walk through this life together. He did it. Did I do anything to deserve His unconditional love or her hand in marriage? Absolutely not. He did it because He loved me first.

1 Jn 4:19: "We love because he first loved us."

We love because He first loved us and he will not withhold any good thing from us. He gives exceedingly abundantly above all we can ask or think (*Eph 3:20-21*):

> *"Now to him who is able to do exceedingly abundantly more than all we ask or think, according to his power that is at work within us..."*

And *2 Peter 1:3-4*:

> *"His divine power has given to us all things that pertain to life and godliness, through the knowledge of Him who called us by glory and virtue, by which have been given to us exceedingly great and precious promises, that through these you may be partakers of the divine nature, having escaped the corruption that is in the world through lust."*

Now if that isn't extravagant love, then I don't know what is. Amen.

Eric Ingram
Co-CEO 100 Fold Life Productions
Wendy's Husband, Spirit-Mate, & Biggest Fan

Table of Contents

Introduction

If you have been in a relationship with God for any length of time, you are aware of the different seasons and stages of that relationship with Him. From surrendering your life to him and acknowledging him as your Lord and Savior to becoming a servant dying to yourself and wanting to serve others, to becoming a warrior by being obedient and using and maintaining your authority when warring in the spirit. However, there is more. Becoming his bride means going deeper and learning the intimacy of God, then ruling and reigning from a place of Love as HIS QUEEN. See I always saw myself as the 'woman at the well' needing to be saved or the girl with the alabaster box grateful and willing to give Him my everything. I saw myself with Mary sitting at his feet soaking in him, but he wanted more. He wanted more than just obedience and gratefulness; He wanted my whole heart, intimacy, true Love. He wanted me to become like Ruth, the Shulamite woman, and his queen, Esther, and most importantly, Him, my first love (*Rev 2:4*).

From the sword to the scepter is my encounter with God. After 18 years in ministry and serving God, He met me in my dreams and asked me to go deeper. Deeper than I could've ever imagined with my human brain. In this book, I am going to share with you my intimate accounts with the Lord that led me to not only become more intimate with him, but to know my authority in the spirit and how to access it, not through warring, but through that same intimacy. My prayer is that through my transparency you will be able to go to this deep inner place within yourself where only HIS true love resides. Our conversation went something like this:

"You don't know me, you don't receive me as your husband."
"Faith I have. Grace I receive. Your promises I know to be true."

But somehow I forgot to ask. Somehow I failed to see Him standing right in front of me as my bridegroom longing for my hand in marriage and to grant me my hearts desires. Up to half his kingdom. I always saw myself in the kitchen, like Martha, the servant girl. Here he is, some 18 years later, standing right in front of me weeping and saying,

"Why won't you receive Me?" "Why don't you allow me to love you?"
"Why have you never asked me for anything of your heart's desire"?

I stood there in utter shock. I grieved Him. I hurt Him. How is this possible, God? What have I done? I have honored him; I have surrendered to him; I have tried to obey his commandments, maybe not perfectly, maybe not all at once, but how did I walk right past Him and not see his hand reaching out to me? How can I receive extravagant love when I see myself as a filthy rag or a forsaken child? His love is so rich it will literally take over your very being. But if you're broken and you can't see yourself past the pain, the bruises and the scars, you may miss his extravagant love and life that he has intended for you:
He made you in his image.

> *Gen 1:27: "So God created mankind in his own image, in the image of God he created them, male and female he created."*

He created all parts of you.

> *Ps 139:13 NLT You made all the delicate, inner parts of my body and knit me together in my mother's womb.*

You are lovable because God is love and you are made in his image.

> *1 Jn 4:8 He that loveth not knoweth not God, for God is LOVE.*

You are beautiful.

> *Song of Solomon 4:7 "You are altogether beautiful, my darling, and there is no blemish in you.*

You are hidden.

> *Col 3:3 "For you died to this life, and your real life is hidden with Christ in God."*

So if you are saved, you died to the old version of yourself. You are now hidden in Christ Jesus. Amen!? So if you are listening to anyone other than God about who you are, you're not hearing the truth, because only through Christ can others see the new you.

His Grace he gives to me freely.

Imagine you are locked in a cell and that you are given a set of keys that not only unlock that cell, but opens the door to a whole, free, healed and prosperous life. You are priceless to God! So much so that he impregnated a virgin just to borne His son, pure and without sin, and allowed him to be beaten and killed *for you*! He loved you so much, He had that same son, Jesus Christ, spend three days in hell so he could take back the keys for eternal life. That's how in love God is with you!

> *Rev 1:18: "I am the Living One; I was dead, and now look, I am alive for ever and ever! And I hold the keys of death and Hades."*

Those keys not only paid for your sins, they unlocked the doors to the earthly cell and freed you! Those same keys also allow you to open the door to His mansion and to sit at his feet to dance with him, to eat with him, to praise His Holy Name. "Holy-Holy-Holy is the Lord God Almighty."

Mt 16:19: "I will give you the keys of the kingdom of heaven; whatever you bind on earth will be bound in heaven, and whatever you loose on earth will be loosed in heaven. They are the keys to victory: faith, hope, and love. And love key is the greatest of

Day 1: Love Affair

The words I write are not to bring condemnation nor guilt, but to restore your life. To strengthen the bonds of your inheritance from generation to generation. Our *sole* purpose on earth is not to acquire all the riches upon it, but to strengthen the *soul* ties to each other and win back the inheritance of the Lord.

> *1 Jn 3:8: "The one who does what is sinful is of the devil, because the devil has been sinning from the beginning. The reason the Son of God appeared was to destroy the devil's work."*

Our purpose is to win back his trust, to build our faith, and to fall deeply in love with our Maker so that with each generation, Satan will lose more ground, more resources, and more souls, and the kingdom of God becomes strengthened and restored unto God his holy nation.

Why then do we seek mysterious buried treasure, untold riches, land, and unexpected wins such as lottery's and so forth?

I feel it's because we are yearning for greater things that we know we lost the day Adam and Eve ate that apple. It's not material possessions were lusting after specifically, but it's everything we lost when we became sinners: the intimacy, the peace, the rest, the completeness, wholeness and the blessed connection with God, our creator.

Gen 3: 8-9: "Then the man and his wife heard the sound of the Lord God as he was walking in the garden in the cool of the day, and they hid from the Lord God among the trees of the garden. But the Lord God called to the man, "Where are you?"

Lev 26:12: "I will walk among you and be your God, and you will be my people."

Deut 31:6: "Be strong and courageous. Do not be afraid or terrified because of them, for the Lord your God goes with you; he will never leave you nor forsake you."

The legacy we need to acquire, the inheritance we need to restore is our passionate, unrelenting love with our Maker. Let's teach this generation-in love, truth, passion and intimacy-how to impart into the next generation without leaving behind the previous one. Let's stay connected and aware of the strategies of the enemy coming against us. Let's fight together in one accord regardless of where we live, who we are, or the color of our skin. We are all from the same creator. A spectacular maker who wove us together like a fine cloth to create a beautiful pattern of life, love and liberty, a true inheritance, the remnant of our king. So let's begin together. Let's start to shift our minds to think like Him. Imagine what it was like in paradise.

What would happen if we all shifted our hearts and minds at once by taking our rightful place with God and within the body of Christ? What would happen if we chose to completely walk in love, choosing to truly love everyone? Or what if for one day, one hour, or even just for one moment, we all stop, drop and refocus? Stop our own thoughts and selfish agendas. Stop competing, arguing, and fighting with one another.

What would happen if we dropped our weapons, our defense mechanisms, and our biases and refocused our thoughts to his? What if for one moment, everyone on Earth stopped and said the name, *Jesus*, in the softest whisper and took Him into their heart and bound the enemy in His name? What would this tremendous moment be like? Would the sky open up and the Glory of the Lord shine a warm, yet vibrant ray of sunshine that would warm each of us to the core, heal our hearts, our wounds, our souls? Would we see satan fall? Would we hear his screams of defeat? Would we see his legends of demons fall to their knees and repent to the true living God?

Would angels fill the skies? Or better yet, would the angels living among us reveal themselves to us? What if your neighbors, coworkers, friends, transients, or that bratty kid were actual angels in-disguise? For the first time since we were born, we would catch a momentary glimpse of the whole truth and nothing but the truth. Would there be a soft trickling rain of our Father's tears saying, "Come, come to me, my beautiful children?"

As I even write this, tears are welling up inside me. That for one brief moment we would have peace, this incredible, mind-blowing sense of comfort, calmness, and complete fearlessness. No child would be harmed, no crimes committed, no death, sickness, not even hurt or anger. Every question would be answered so no doubt could exist. Just total awareness of our life, our Father, and his complete love. Would our senses become totally alive? Would we would see colors more vivid and vibrant? Would food taste heavenly sweet? Would our hearing become crisper, keener? Our touch more tactile? Our feelings more palpable and reticent?

I would love to see in the years to come that we've evolved into more caring, compassionate, and impassioned human beings with the greatest outflow of love and empathy this world's never seen. It would be too powerful to contain. Nations could heal nations, becoming truly brothers in love. We would care more about the freedom of others than ourselves. We'd stand for virtue at all cost and leave the past, the pain and the hurts behind. The heart of it all is to know that everyone created is created in the exact image of God. When we get past the flesh and concentrate on the soul, we will see we are all the same. We are God's. His lost sheep. His beloved. HIS. Who then are we to hate, hurt, or even try to kill anyone? We should embrace everyone. We must love them and truly care for them. I'm not suggesting to love people's bad actions or the false teachings they've been indoctrinated with, but to love their souls. See past their exteriors, man-made walls and masks. See the very core of their being and then speak right to it.

Teach them, love them, accept them, and yes, pray for them more than yourself. The soul is the treasure God is truly longing for. It's the very essence of this journey we are encamped on. His focus is not circumstances, rights, nor laws, but on restoration-returning your heart back to His. No one should perish; no one should die without the knowledge of who He as their Father, Son and Holy Spirit. Wow, what a moment in time. What a truly breathtaking moment that would be if we could all be in one accord, one heartbeat, one mind focused on heaven and him at the exact same time. That would become the most incredible love affair that the Lord has ever known.

Now that we know that the love affair-the intimacy-is what he longs for, we have to identify the difference between the types of love: true intimacy, passion and lust.

So many Christians are focused on the laws of the bible, which are important to have knowledge of. However, it does not negate the love we are commanded to have not only for one another, but toward God, our husband, as well as for ourselves. We can never truly love without grace and we can't truly give grace without loving. The key is the

LOVE. True love and intimacy is not wrong or bad. It's necessary to bring healing to lost and fallen world. So let's start this journey together by defining the types of love:

Physical Love - EROS
Erotic, sensual, intimacy, the drawing of one to another in becoming one flesh. A safe haven of rest between a husband and his wife where they can find wholeness, rest and restoration.

Family Love - STORGE
Love between a parent and their children, family. Creates bonding and a connection used for growth and nurturing as well. Thriving occurs.

Affectionate Love - PHILIO
Warm-hearted, compassionate, brotherly love

Action, Selfless Love - AGAPE
Self no longer exists and only a true love without selfish gain can be achieved. It's a commitment and honor God has towards us, complete, whole. Not attached to emotions.
It's God perfected in us. It's the Love of *1 Cor 13:1-13*:

"If I speak in the tongues[a] of men or of angels, but do not have love, I am only a resounding gong or a clanging cymbal. If I have the gift of prophecy and can fathom all mysteries and all knowledge, and if I have a faith that can move mountains, but do not have love, I am nothing. If I give all I possess to the poor and give over my body to hardship that I may boast,[b] but do not have love, I gain nothing. Love is patient, love is kind. It does not envy, it does not boast, it is not proud. It does not dishonor others, it is not self-seeking, it is not easily angered, it keeps no record of wrongs. Love does not delight in evil but rejoices with the truth. It always protects, always trusts, always hopes, always perseveres. Love never fails. But where there are prophecies, they will cease; where there are tongues, they will be stilled; where there is knowledge, it will pass away. For we know in part and we prophesy in part, but when completeness comes, what is in part disappears. When I was a child, I talked like a child, I thought like a child, I reasoned like a child.

When I became a man, I put the ways of childhood behind me. For now we see only a reflection as in a mirror; then we shall see face to face. Now I know in part; then I shall know fully, even as I am fully known. And now these three remain: faith, hope and love. But the greatest of these is love.

Another illustration was when God asked Peter in *Jn 21:15-19*:

"After breakfast, Jesus said to Simon Peter, "Simon, son of John, do you love me more than these?" "Yes, Master, you know I love you." Jesus said, "Feed my lambs." He then asked a second time, "Simon, son of John, do you love me?" "Yes, Master, you know I love you." Jesus said, "Shepherd my sheep." Then he said it a third time: "Simon, son of John, do you love me?" Peter was upset that he asked for the third time, "Do you love me?" so he answered, "Master, you know everything there is to know. You've got to know that I love you." Jesus said, "Feed my sheep. I'm telling you the very truth now: When you were young you dressed yourself and went wherever you wished, but when you get old you'll have to stretch out your hands while someone else dresses you and takes you where you don't want to go." He said this to hint at the kind of death by which Peter would glorify God. And then he commanded, "Follow me."

Scripture Meditation: 1 John

Lesson: Everything you want need and desire was placed in you before you were in your mother's womb (*Jer 1:5*):
1. God is always on time. His plans are for you never against you.
2. Do not give into fear, keep your eyes on Him.
3. Take time to rest in His presence, to soak and to receive the peace that comes from the Holy Spirit.
4. Enjoy the process of becoming a woman, a complete and whole woman before your King is given to you.
5. Trust even in the dark times and the wilderness times.
6. God is always behind the scenes working out the details, stay your course.

Rate yourself in each area of love 1 - 10.

Which ones are you strong in?

Which ones are you weakest in?

How can you improve in each type of love in your daily life?

Day 2: The Lion at the River...

Written By Wendy Darline, 1995

This battle has been long. The enemy has been relentless. I am losing my footing so I press my feet deep into the soil and lift my sword ready to give the final blow. I feel ten more on either side of me fast approaching. I have lost many soldiers in this fight, but I must not give in. As I draw my sword up over my head, I hear a mighty thunderous roar. I find strength. And with all my might I let out a yell and submit the final blow. It is done! He is defeated. The remaining have fled in every direction afraid of the one who let out that thunderous roar.

Worn from the battle, but determined to make it back home, I continue to press on over the hills. I can see it in the distance, my home. The memories of Him and his love cause tears to burn down my face like liquid lava staining my dirty and worn face. I can not wait to see you, to touch you, and to hear your voice that is soothing music to my weary soul. I approached the river of living water. It looks so clear, so beautiful, and so radiant. I bend down to take a drink and see my disheveled self. I begin to drink and splash my face with the cool water. Grateful and very thankful to be nearing home, my hope is what has kept me going while my faith kept me alive. You are my beloved who I love more than life itself and am honored to serve you and our kingdom. You are and have been my strength, my love and my King. I long to be inhabited by you once more. My soul begins to desire you and to allow myself to feel again knowing that I am safe in passage and nearing the gates to our home.

As my spirit connects with his, I hear the roar of the lion. It sends chills up my spine and makes my body come alive. He must sense I am near. I begin to giggle like a schoolgirl. His roar is loud and thunderous and keeps the evil at bay. Men tremble. And those around Him who don't know Him are in fear. But for me it is soothing and comforting. I look closer at the reflection of myself in the lake wondering if there's any hope in cleaning myself up to be presentable enough to come into his presence prior to the banquet.

I begin to lift my dress to put my feet into the water when I feel his breath on the nape of my neck. I look down into the water and see his long mane and his lovely eyes staring at me with love. I turn quickly to see his face and to wrap my arms around his big strong neck. "Oh how I've missed you," I whisper into his ear. Tears flood both our faces as He nuzzles his face into my neck and breathed a sigh of relief that I have made it back home again to Him. I bury my face in His mane and just breathe Him in as well. I begin to giggle at him,

"You couldn't even wait for me to get to the house? Will you let me

finish washing so I could look sufficient for you?"

He shakes his head no and begins to lick my face. Your love is so captivating, so bold, it leaves me breathless and longing for more. You have my heart and my soul. I love you and long for you deeply. I fall deeper and deeper for you with each return. I sit down at the side of the river and you lay next to me. As I begin sharing my journey and treacherous battles with you, you begin to lick the wounds on my hands, face and neck. As you breathe on me and nuzzle me, I take my hand and raise it toward your powerful face and rub your soft cheek. I feel the warm tears flowing from your eyes,

"I missed you, too," I whispered.

The salt from your tongue begins to cleanse and purify my wounds. You know how I love you. And the more I grow, the more I war. The more I change, the deeper my love for you becomes. Nothing stays the same, yet, you are always so near to me. So familiar to me. Deep calls to Deep.

As you begin to purr, my heart heals. The weariness from battle dissipates from me and my body becomes whole and full of life again. As you lay your head upon your paws, I slip back into the water to finish washing. I descend underwater letting it quench my head, face and body. My head emerges from the water. I see you looking at me, smiling. So I giggle and playfully begin splashing your face with the water. You rise up and let out a gentle roar with all your hair standing on end. I can see the playfulness in your eyes. I come up out of the water refreshed and more alive. My wet clothes cling to my body as goosebumps form on my skin from the cool breeze. I throw my arms around you and we nuzzle once more.

As we lay down, the warm sun begins to dry me. I reach up to scratch you behind the ear in tenderness and affection feeling your loving embrace and feeling so very safe. I begin to sing songs of love to

13

you. My gratitude for you and for us is overwhelming to me. I know you are happy because your mane is sitting up and is full. Your purring becomes deeper as you lay next to me. Your ear is inclined to me and is taking in every word and melody. Oh how captivating our love is. Right now, nothing else matters. Nothing else exists. I know you long for these times as much as I do, if not more.

As you lick my face and smooth my hair with your paws, we just enjoy the scent and feel of each other. Abandoned for one another in love and harmony. My wounds are no longer visible, but my strength and my beauty have returned... because of your love for me. I just lay and sigh, "Wow, what a journey. What a war." It was worth it, and when I ends, it always brings me back to you better and more complete than before. My rest is in you.

As we lay there on the hill near the river, I begin to hear the voices of the troops he had sent in to gather the wounded and all of the spoil. The enemy was not only defeated, but completely stripped of everything he took and more. I also hear the voice of the handmaidens signing songs of jubilee as they gather the food for tonight's celebration. He always has a banquet to celebrate my return, to rejoice at the victory and to give glory. As the honored guest, He will serve me and invite the enemy to come and give me honor over the battle won. Restoration comes to his warriors as the defeated have to come back to admit their defeat. He honors me, decrees my new name, my new mantle, gives out the orders and the precepts and establishes me and my kingdom for him, all in presence of the enemy. The lion, my lion, is strong. He's definitely the King. His roar rumbles like thunder and he demands respect. He is strong and able and fully confident. He is my protector and he causes the enemy to tremble at my feet.

Sometimes I forget how strong he is because he is so tender to me. The fire in his eyes and the thunder of his roar lets the enemy know when it's enough and they flee. Every knee bows when the King nears. I close my eyes and meditate on him and begin dreaming....

then I am awoken by a maiden who has come to bring us substance for us to commune one with another. Bread and wine are left as she smiles and quickly leaves. Another brings a robe for me. Another, shoes for my feet. I take the bread, tear it, and dip it first into the wine. We bow our heads and close our eyes and give thanks. I feed him first, and then take a bite for myself. I stand to begin undressing and putting on my new garments. As I do, the lion stands to leave so he too can prepare for tonight. I touch his cheek and say," See you soon," and He is off.

As quick as he came, he leaves out of sight. My body, so light and carefree and better than before, is quick to receive my new clothes. I begin adorning myself for tonight. As always I feel so loved and cared for. He tended to me so perfectly. He spoke to my heart, tended to my wounds and refreshed my soul. My lover is so good to me. The taste of the communion is still on my lips and filled the void in both my spirit and my stomach. He always meets every need. Everything is always better than before.

My carriage awaits for the remainder of my journey back home. This part is where I finish my rest and come into the palace to receive my good fortune, my spoils, my abundance, as well as my time of celebration for him and for his Kingdom. My privilege and my honor to daily give to him is rewarded beyond measure. He never ceases to amaze me.

Lesson: Know when to war, when to be still, and when the battle is over:
1. He is our vindicator.
2. Know he never leaves you nor forsakes you.
3. Remember to return to being a woman once the war is over.
4. God is always on your side there to love you support you and to prepare a banquet for you in front of you enemies.

You are never warring against people. You are, however, warring against your thoughts and emotions. You are engaged in a battle in and for the mind. The enemy is smart enough not to come big and bold in the natural, but he's a master at planting seeds of doubt.

Scripture Meditation:

*"Cast your cares on the Lord
and he will sustain you;
he will never let
the righteous be shaken." Ps 55:22*

*"The wicked flee tho no one pursues, but the righteous are
as bold as a Lion." Prov.28:1*

*"They will follow the Lord, he will roar like a mighty Lion. When he roars
his children will come trembling from the west." Hos 11:10*

*"Wherever you hear the sound of the trumpet, join us there.
Our God will fight for us." Neh 4:20*

All while restoring you.

*"And I will restore to you the years that the locust hath eaten, the
cankerworm, and the caterpiller, and the palmerworm, my great army
which I sent among you." Joel 2:25*

Day 3: The Healing Rooms

Written By Wendy Darline, 1996

Down the great hall just past the banquet room is a set of doors that lead to creativity. On the doors carved in the wood, it says "Where Love Resides." Upon opening the doors, you see He is a creator, full of life and creativity. There are canvases everywhere, paints brushes, clay, sculptures, easels, note pads, sketch pads, pencils, chalks, and every color you could possibly imagine and more. My King is an amazing talent of life. He creates everything with such purpose and intent. Complete masterpieces, each unique and very different, yet, all in his own likeness and in his image. Every detail so carefully laid out. He presents it in such a way that the world sometimes can't even see it in its completeness or its magnitude.

Our natural eyes can't obtain all the beauty of the King unless He opens your eyes in such a way as to give you a spiritual glimpse of the life we live from His sight and not our own limited view. Color is everywhere on the walls, the floors and even on his hands. The air is filled with gentle fragrances that inspire his creativity and the sound of music swims around the room creating life and love in the atmosphere. It all inspires him.

At this very moment, He's creating something brand new and restoring something he once created by adding new colors and aspects to its already existing form. His masterpieces continue to evolve and grow as they take on their identity, weather difficult times and become more experienced through time and space. They each have been given to someone as a gift. They have been carefully and methodically planned for the execution of his will and his timing for that particular heritage and purpose. As a declaration of his love and his beauty, he creates a new piece, a new life, fulfills a new promise. Every stroke of His brush tells of his story, of his life breathed into their being, showing his creativity in every work.

He always knows its purpose, its destiny. He stands back looking at the completed work from its conception, knowing his delight will be fulfilled in and through each piece. Nothing is impossible for Him. His heart's desire is woven into every creative miracle. So much meticulous thought and care goes into each piece and the receiver of the gift. His pieces are never for sale, but always a gift. He knows exactly who they are for as he designs them. As he puts the brush to the canvas and begins to create, He knows the journey it will travel. He knows their thoughts, their hopes and their desires. He puts into each piece everything that it will need to be able to live and complete its purpose, its destiny.

Ps 37:4: "Take delight in the Lord,
and he will give you the desires of your heart."

As you walk past this main area, you see massive doors that lead to individual rooms. Behind each door and in each room are very distinct fragrances, foods and drinks. These are healing rooms where each masterpiece comes to find rest, refreshing and restoration. Sometimes they come back just to see him, their creator so they can show of their wear. He touches them up, relishes at His work, or just welcomes their surprise visit. Every created miracle knows how to find this place and how to come back from that which they were created. Whether it's a chip, a crack, weather-beaten, torn or losing its color, our creator desires us to come back in and be restored. Some come utterly shattered and unrecognizable, but not to Him. He knows who you are. He will heal them and leave them refreshed and revitalized so that they continue to be the very beauty and splendor of their King.

He never grows tired of his work or maintaining what he has already created. He loves it. It makes him whole and complete. Some call this place 'the potter house.' Some call it 'the master's place.' Whatever you may call it, everyone knows this is where you come to sit with your creator and receive a touch from him. Over the years, I have visited this place often. His touch is always needed. His power is overwhelming and his love is complete and totally satisfying. There's power in his touch and healing in his love for each of us.

He heals me, restores me, in fact, he has even transformed me to where I couldn't even recognize my own image or reflection. Over the years I had been abused, mishandled, and even shattered past recognition. All of the work of man and wars caused breakage, tearing and fading of my colors sometimes causing me to not recognize myself or remember my purpose. I would need to come to the master for a touch up, a repurposing, or a complete transformation. Always better than before. His creations are definitely His. He takes great pride in each and every one of them.

He always greets me with a smile. He is always so careful to welcome me with refreshments, wine, cakes, fruit and honey. New living water that can quench not only my thirst, but breath hope and faith back into my very dry bones. He is a man of details. He is always such the perfectionist in everything he does, says or gives to you. It's always exactly what you need at the exact moment you need it. Most of the time you never even knew that it was missing or that you are in need of it.

He fixes what's broken, removes what's damaged, and sometimes replaces things that are missing. He talks to you about your journey, carefully listening to your heart to know its beat and to be able to share how you have come out of the battle stronger, better, more complete. He eases your pain, takes all your burdens and fills you to overflowing with the abundance of new life. Over the years this has become more relevant than ever. My very soul cries out for this time with him where I can be transformed and cared for in a way that only my creator can and does. For He knew me before. He breaks bread with me. He grounds me and embraces me in love, joy and peace. He finds humor for me, rejoices over my victories and cries with me over my losses. He truly cares for me and enjoys seeing my growth, my journey and my destiny fulfilled.

The rooms are calm and peaceful, full of his love and life and splendor. He always has one ready for you when you come and it will always have exactly what you are in need of down to the last detail. There's a place to rest your head, oils for healing, fragrances to open up your heart and mind, drinks to satisfy your thirst, fresh manna to feed your spirit, music that will sooth you and restore love and peace. As you lay there soaking in his presence, He will begin gently stroking you with his paint brush as to restore and refresh and revitalize the masterpiece in you. Your soul will be touched and your spirit will be quenched as you're transformed again for his glory and delight. The splendor of your King.

Most of the time you think you're coming for one thing, but the beauty of your King is he knows what you are in need of and will take care of all your needs. My room today is dimly lit with pillows of warm chocolate brown and teal blue like the foam from the sea. The material draped over them is smooth like silk, cool and refreshing to my skin. There is a table with wine, chocolates, fruits and cakes for my eating. There are bottles of water, oil, and fragrances for my hair and for the wounds on my body that still remain from the battle. I also see a bottle of milk and a jar of honey. My mind knows I am in need of some reminding of hopes and dreams.

Off in the corner is a beautiful angelic being sitting on a stool, ebony with long black braids. The sash across her chest says, "Reader, Comforter." She will speak His word to me, the very word He has prepared my heart to receive on this day. I sigh, it was a long haul a rough battle to get here, but I made it. And as always, he's prepared for me. My mind can't wonder; I am fixed on him. I gently take off my worn clothes, wash my feet and hands, and slip into the silky sheets for a much needed nap. As I lay there, she begins to read to me, ministering first to my ears, then my mind, then my heart and then my spirit. I feel sleepy, relaxed and ready to receive all that he has for me. He is near. I feel his presence. As I lay waiting, I do feel some anticipation for his arrival. Knowing he has made this appointment with me and cared for every detail, planning for me, I can't help but be excited to see him. The One who created me, who loves me.

As time goes by, my excitement builds, my emotions heighten. I feel overwhelmed with love and gratitude. The aroma in the air gets thicker, more pungent. The fragrances of honeysuckle, lavender and gardenias fill my nostrils. I hear the gentle strums of harps and violins. He serenades me; his affection thickens the atmosphere with the scent of love and intimacy. I'm reminded of the day he created me. It's taking me back to when I first met him, "Oh God, how I love Him, because he first loved me."

He now enters the room. The stage has been set. His presence brings me to a place of which my whole being can receive him. I sit up ready to greet him with a kiss, to share with him, to commune with him and be satisfied. His hands are strong; his eyes are loving; and his stature is so big and powerful, yet, he is always so tender and kind, gentle in every way. I am completely trusting and completely loving him. We embrace. Carefully he touches me and carefully he listens to me. He knows me; I am alive again. Worn from my travels, scarred from my battles, weary from my trials, I am instantly healed, instantly whole, because he loves me. With each stroke of his paint brush, my beauty returns. The areas that had become faded and torn are no more. I marvel at the restoration of me.

While he smooths out the rough spots, fills in all the cracks, we talk and laugh and rejoice with one another in perfect joy and harmony. My Maker, My Creator, loves me. I continue to eat, drink and just laugh with him. All the while I can't even feel the work he is doing to restore me. He pulls out a mirror for me to take a peek. A tear runs down my cheek. "Better than before," I say to him. He takes the mirror from my hand, kisses me gently on the forehead and says, "Now stay awhile, rest, sleep." He's made me whole, like brand new... He truly first loved me.

I linger in this quiet place surrounded by his goodness, his tenderness and mercy. I breathe Him in me and fall into a restful nap. As I awake from my respite, I see he has prepared gifts for me. He has given me things the enemy had taken from me, plus so much more than I needed or required. He freely gives me. I just wanted to see him. He's the only gift I ever need. Yet he always gives to me. He leaves me totally and completely satisfied: My Artist, Creator, King and Lover of my soul. He loves me.

Scripture Meditation:

> *Heb 4:16: "Let us then approach God's throne of grace with confidence, so that we may receive mercy and find grace to help us in our time of need."*

Ps 23:
"The LORD *is my shepherd, I lack nothing.*
He makes me lie down in green pastures,
he leads me beside quiet waters,
he refreshes my soul.
He guides me along the right paths
for his name's sake.
Even though I walk
through the darkest valley, [a]
I will fear no evil,
for you are with me;
your rod and your staff,
they comfort me.
You prepare a table before me
in the presence of my enemies.
You anoint my head with oil;
my cup overflows.
Surely your goodness and love will follow me
all the days of my life,
and I will dwell in the house of the LORD
forever."

Lesson: His mercy and grace abound for all who ask.

Day 4: The Dance

Written By Wendy Darline, 2001

Tonight is my night with the King. As I received my summons, my heart flutters with anxious anticipation, excited for what's to come. I began to prepare. First, the music. I selected songs with the melody of harps, flutes, violins and more string instruments. Second, I prepare a bath. As I fill it with warm water, I start adding fragrances: lilac, frankincense and myrrh, the scents of the King. I slip out of my bed clothes and descend into the tepid water and began to soak. I lay back and take a deep, lung-cleansing breath. I close my eyes and begin daydreaming of times before with my King. The moments we've shared together remind me of His love. I feel His presence. I feel His strong and mighty hands in my hair as He begins to pour the water over me. It gently trickles down my back. He begins massaging my scalp and washing my hair. I feel so loved, refreshed and cared for. He lifts the pitcher of water above my head and begins rinsing the soap from my hair.

When He finishes, He leans close to my ears and whispers His love to me and kisses my forehead. My King, so strong, bold, and confident, makes you want to listen to every word He speaks. When He gives me direction or correction, I do everything in my power to bring myself into alignment. It's never in a way that makes me cringe or get defensive. I love Him so much; I yearn for His approval, His love, His tenderness. I need it. I can't live without it.

Just as quick as He came, He left to prepare for our evening. Realizing the time, I lift my relaxed and completely restored body out of the tub and begin drying myself off. I saunter toward my closet to prepare for this night, thinking of what to wear. I turn to the right and out of the corner of my eye, I spy on the armchair an exquisite gown laced with jewels and sewn with strands of silver and gold thread laid out for me. This royal purple gown looks fit for a queen. He thinks of everything. Excited to please Him and make Him feel special, I gladly slip on the extravagant dress. Aaah, the silky fabric feels amazing against my skin. He always seems to find ways in the smallest of details to make me feel beautiful, unique and extraordinarily His.

My ladies-in-waiting come in to do the final touches, oil my feet and hands and style my hair with tendrils and curls that excite my King. I admire my body bedazzled with jewels in the mirror. I imagine His fingers in my hair, twirling it around His strong fingers. Again my mind wanders to our extravagant times before. As the ladies set the crown upon my head, I am reminded that tonight there is no war. Tonight, I am not preparing for battle. Tonight, I am his crown of glory, his spoil. Tonight, I am the bride of a King. I sigh as I take one last look in the mirror and smile. He will be pleased knowing He is my gift and I am His.

I make my way down the stairs and out through the main corridors. I enter into the great hall. To the left is a window that looks out in His inner courtyard. To the right leads me to the house of prayer and the banquet hall. I stand alone in the great hall that leads into the celebratory hall and the grand ballroom. In front of me are two large gold doors with carvings of cherubs, fruit trees and vineyards like a beautiful mural or painting. It tells a story of His home, His passion, His heritage. I'm bubbling with anticipation to see what He has prepared for us this evening. My King is sentimental, always the gentleman. Many know of Him, but few really know Him. He is full of love, passion and sensitivity, yet, strong and superbly courageous. He rules from a place of knowledge and compassion, not from a place of fear or anger.

I take a deep breath and prepare to enter in. The doors open wide and I see the room has been transformed once again. All of the tables and chairs have been removed and in the middle of the room is a giant tent. There are tables with fruits and desserts and fine wine, romantic and endearing down to the colors of the curtains, the soft pillows and the delectable array of fruits and wines. Pillows line one side of the floor and as I look down at my feet, petals of flowers line the floor. Candles are flickering with luminous orange-gold flames. The air is saturated with astonishingly pungent aromas and the pitch-perfect harmony of singing angels. Again He has outdone himself. I continue to absorb the whole picture so that it will stay etched in my mind longer than this night.

He is near. My body begins to yearn for His touch, His smile and His sweet, gentle breath upon my neck. Then, I see Him. He's staring at me with awe. It's like the first time we met *every time*. He peers right into my heart and soul. He loves me so deeply and with such desire that I know my King's heart is for me. He takes me by the hand and feeds me a fig. We drink some wine, and then, we dance. He escorts me to the center of the floor. All eyes are on us as we embrace. He leads me like He always does. We are the perfect couple on the floor. Much like our life together, we fit. We complement one another.

Our bodies flow to the rhythm. Our hearts are synchronized to each other. My body craves His and he mine. He pulls me into him deeper so that you can't see where He stops and I start. He whirls me around the floor, whispering love songs in my ear. His words penetrate my soul and bring complete healing to my every wound, fear or fleshly need.

He knows I am completely and utterly in love with him. I tell him my thoughts towards him and he comes alive with emotions and wants. His desire is for me. My king, My king, oh how I adore my King and he adores me. Time stands still. I swear he winds back the clocks so that this night together can last for eternity. God loves you. He knows the many trials and battles you've gone through. That's why he desires to meet you on that dance floor: to worship, to praise and to rejoice.

Rate yourself in each area of love 1 - 10.
Which ones are you strong in?
Which ones are you weakest in?
How can you improve in each type of love?

Lesson:

The dance shows us how to complement one another, to trust one another. It gives our bodies understanding of one another and helps our souls to become one. It teaches our flesh to be still, to feel complete and lack for nothing. It causes intimacy to grow and understanding, knowledge, and yes, wisdom to flow. The dance also teaches us when and how to move for one another and how to make room for one another. It causes us to trust each other for the next step.

Scripture Meditation:

Zeph 3:17:
"The Lord your God in your midst,
The Mighty One, will save;
He will rejoice over you with gladness,
He will quiet you with His love,
He will rejoice over you with singing."

Ps 149:3 — "Let them praise his name in the dance: let them sing
praises unto him with the timbrel and harp."

Ps 150:4 — "Praise him with the timbrel and dance: praise him with
stringed instruments and organs."

Jer 31:13 — "Then shall the virgin rejoice in the dance, both young men and
old together: for I will turn their mourning into joy, and will comfort them,
and make them rejoice from their sorrow."

2 Sam 6:14 — "And David danced before the LORD with all [his] might;
and David [was] girded with a linen ephod."

Ps 150:1 - 127:6 — "Praise ye the LORD. Praise God in his sanctuary:
praise him in the firmament of his power."

Ps 30:11 — "Thou hast turned for me my mourning into dancing: thou
hast put off my sackcloth, and girded me with gladness."

Ps 149:1 - 127:9 — "Praise ye the LORD. Sing unto the LORD a new song,
[and] his praise in the congregation of saints."

Eccl 3:4 — "A time to weep, and a time to laugh; a time to mourn,
and a time to dance..."

Ex 15:20 — "And Miriam the prophetess, the sister of Aaron, took a timbrel
in her hand; and all the women went out after her with timbrels and
with dances."

Ps 150:3 - 127:5 — "Praise him with the sound of the trumpet: praise him with the psaltery and harp."

Col 3:17 — "And whatsoever ye do in word or deed, [do] all in the name of the Lord Jesus, giving thanks to God and the Father by him."

Jer 31:4 — "Again I will build thee, and thou shalt be built, O virgin of Israel: thou shalt again be adorned with thy tabrets, and shalt go forth in the dances of them that make merry."

Jn 4:24 — "God [is] a Spirit: and they that worship him must worship [him] in spirit and in truth."

Jn 4:23 — "But the hour cometh, and now is, when the true worshippers shall worship the Father in spirit and in truth: for the Father seeketh such to worship him."

1 Chr 15:29 — "And it came to pass, [as] the ark of the covenant of the LORD came to the city of David, that Michal the daughter of Saul looking out at a windowsaw king David dancing and playing: and she despised him in her heart."

2 Sam 6:12-16 — "And it was told king David, saying, The LORD hath blessed the house of Obededom, and all that [pertaineth] unto him, because of the ark of God. So David went and brought up the ark of God from the house of Obededom into the city of David with gladness."

Day 5: The Courtroom

Written by: Wendy Darline   11/8/1999

Our covenant with God...

Piled on the table higher than the eye can see are stacks and stacks of papers, legal forms, law books, scrolls and tablets, documentation with notes salutations, scribbles and highlighted portions. Alongside the table is a weights and measures scale. It's amazing to see the ledgers, the records of every wrong you have committed. To see in writing your mistakes, bad choices and vengeful deeds recorded against you. If you saw an account of every word you ever spoke-both good and bad-would you speak differently? Regardless, according to the world's standards, I am guilty. I am less than perfect. Have I committed worse sins than others? Possibly. Have others committed worse sins than me? Most definitely. However, it's all sin in the eyes of the court. As I look through each pile, I see stories of old, decrees of the King, laws of the land, precepts, lineage accounts, historical events, and the Lamb's Book of Life. It's not just about me, it's about my heritage and bloodline as well.

The Opposition enters the courtroom with his hands full of rules, laws, post-it notes with dates and times of every event and situation I mishandled, ever. They call him 'The Liar,' 'The Thief.' He thinks he's in charge. He's followed by an army of 'expert witnesses' who've kept track of my wrongdoings, word curses, vows of dissension and greed. He questions his expert witnesses on the witness stand and one-by-one they proceed to hurl lies, accusations, and slander against my name and character. He is called 'the great accuser' for a reason.

When his litany of liars is finished, he calls me to the stand. After I sit nervously, he begins to throw every bit of my unsavory past in my face, trying with all of his trickery and wiles to provoke me to become angry or offended, hoping I'd grow weary, give up, and declare myself guilty on all charges. He thinks he's going to win my case, but then my life will be his and my soul will be with him for eternity, never again to see daylight or the glory.

He takes great pleasure in reminding me of details he thinks will break me, the bad choices that will make me feel like surrendering. His questions bring about confusion and despair to my mind and spirit. "Have you ever felt remorse for the things you have done, Wendy?," He asks me coyly. "Don't you wish you could go back in time and do it differently now that you can see the situation more... objectively?" But I can't go back in time. I can't undo what we've done. 'So this is it,' I think to myself, I must suffer the consequences of my actions and live with it.

As I'm opening my mouth resolved to condemn myself and seal my fate, my defense team barrels in. My lead attorney strides in wearing a sparkling white badge on his lapel that says, 'High Priest.' He sits at my table and smiles the sweetest, life affirming smile I've ever seen. The bailiff barks, "All bow," as God, the Righteous Judge, takes His high seat. And before The Liar has a chance to speak another lie about me, the High Priest stands up and shows the court the nail hole in the palms of his hands. The Righteous Judge pounds his gavel and yells, "Case dismissed. Wendy Darline, your heart is pure. Your heart I give my mercy to." Amen and Amen!

Scripture Meditation:

> *2 Tim 1:7: "For the Spirit God gave us does not make us timid, but gives us power, love and self-discipline."*

> *Ph 4:6-7: "Do not be anxious about anything, but in every situation, by prayer and petition, with thanksgiving, present your requests to God. And the peace of God, which transcends all understanding, will guard your hearts and your minds*
> *in Christ Jesus."*

> *1 Ptr 4:8: "And above all things have fervent love for one another, for "love will cover a multitude of sins."*

> *Rom 5:8: "But God demonstrates His own love toward us, in that while we were still sinners, Christ died for us."*

Lesson:
Jesus is the Name Above All Names. He is our shield, our protector, our right guard, our shield and buckler. Though there will be trials and tribulations in the world, take heart, for He has overcome the world (*Jn 16:33*).

Day 6: The Banquet

Written by: Wendy Darline 07/21/1987

Desperate to see him and spend time with the one I love, I run towards the outer court to get to the banquet on time. Oh how I miss my lover and want this time with him. The closer I get to the outer court, the more aware I become of my appearance. I begin to straighten out my hair, and smooth out my robe. Oh dear, I know I must look disheveled from both the war and the long journey back home. Oh how I have missed him. I blush with anticipation at seeing his face and feeling his touch. His voice brings me comfort. My body is weary and my strength is depleted. I desperately need to be in his presence in order to feel refreshed, renewed and restored.

 The outer court is made with massive pillars of marble and mark where you enter. From the outer court, you can see the mansion ahead. You see vast fields ripe with fruit and flourishing. Baskets of fruit and grain line the path to the castle. To the left, you see a meadow and a clear running brook, bellowing soft sounds of water crashing against stone that creates a melody of tranquility that refreshes the ears of those who listen intently. To the right, you see the worshipers and the saints giving homage to their King. The servers, too, are giddy while preparing the food and drink for the dinner. The delectable delicacies create an aroma that brings sheer ecstasy to your nostrils while exciting your taste buds with effervescent expectancy for the feast.

I've made it to the gate now and am heading toward the Castle. It's hard rock edges make it appear to be both strong and cold and a force to be reckoned with. The intricacies of the windows draw you closer and make you curious to take a peek inside at what and who might be occupying this dwelling. The mahogany doors are strong and sturdy, each with carvings of the tree of life and cherubs. As I approach, the doors open wide to the inner court. The court is full of fragrant flowers, a brook full of flowing living water, hedges of spices and herbs line the path. The trees are full with the fruits of his labor. I am met by the celebratory staff who know my love for him. They hand me a new robe, adorn my hair and wash my feet. They prepare me to meet him and give him my best. Sweet aromas, like melons, honeydew, and the flower of honeysuckle, fill my hair. I know He will be pleased. I can also hear the harps playing. I feel the atmosphere changing as I approach the Hall. My body feels calm, warm, but my stomach is doing flips and my heart skips a beat...

He is here!!

I feel him before I can even see his shadow. My heart is drawn to him. I hold him in my bosom day and night. I long for these times when I can sit and talk with him and drink with him. To feel His heart toward me and know that he is as anxious to see me. To know He has been waiting for my return day and night, listening for the sound of my voice and the patter of my feet running across the floors of the hall to see him. His heart skips a beat.

The halls are full of the perfume of a great feast prepared just for us. "Taste and see what the Lord has done for me" plays in my head as I approach My King. He welcomes me to the table adorned with goblets of gold and place settings of silver and golds fabrics. Lilacs and purples and golds line the table. A table fit for a king. The table is made of cedar and the walls and floors are lined in pure gold. The pillars throughout the room are made out of the most precious of stones: jasper, onyx, amethyst, sapphire, emerald and more. The table is full of fruits, pomegranates, figs, grapes, peaches, plums, oranges and pears to name a few. Meats are as far as the eye can see. Spices of saffron and spikenard fill the air. There is breads, sweet cakes and filled with figs and raisins. Pitchers of wine in crystal decanters sit upon the table, next to the pots of honey and simmering sauces. It's so good to be home.

He takes me by the hand and leads me to my seat, but not before embracing me, welcoming me back home. He leans in and whispers into my ear, "Job well done, Bride of the Lamb." As I take my seat, I see he is at ease that I have returned. We begin to talk and share our hearts. Entrenched in our conversation, we scarcely realize that we are no longer alone. The table begins to fill with both family and loved ones as well as the enemies I encountered along the way. I am always pleasantly surprised by the guests he invites to dine with us on these intimate nights.

Returning from the battlefield, I always miss family and friends, but he always knows exactly who needs to be with us to celebrate the victory, the reunion, and the triumph. I see the others that he chose to eat with us. Some have taken their rightful seats, others stand in awe, and yet, some are seated on pillows on the floor. Confuse and bewildered I look to him for an explanation. He simply smiles and says, "Some have not yet the faith to take the seat I have prepared for them. I reach out my hand to them in compassion/" Then He gently takes my hand and puts it on his heart and whispers to me, "Come, my beloved, leave them to discover much like you. I long for them to eat with us, however that desire will come from within them. Come sit with me, let's share my darling."

He embraces me, making me feel whole and safe. It allows my body to surrender from the battle and enter into His rest. His touch is full of both passion and power all at once. I know instantly I am wanted, cherished and adored. I walk with him over to the place he has made for me. There are gifts for me at the table, gifts so elaborate to believe: a rare jewel, a feather of many colors like a quill for writing, a banner, a new crown and more. My King, you are so very good to me. I'm so unworthy, yet , I am so full of love for him. I graciously accept them all as they are presented to me and steadfastly listen to the meaning of each. After my gifts are presented, I begin to share my journey and my experiences about his children I encountered along the way. Those I had the opportunity to talk to of him, those I was able to see added to his book and the ones that still need faith to receive him. I love my time in the banquet room with My King.

Later, he tells me of the battle won and the numbers who were saved , we rejoice together over another victory for him. His Kingdom is growing and I love having such a part in it with him. This place here with him is the New Jerusalem, the place of rest and new beginnings.

Rate yourself in each area of love 1 - 10.
Which ones are you strong in?
Which ones are you weakest in?
How can you improve in each type of love?

Scripture Meditation: Lk 14:15-24 (NIV):

The Parable of the Great Banquet

"When one of those at the table with him heard this, he said to Jesus, "Blessed is the one who will eat at the feast in the kingdom of God." Jesus replied: "A certain man was preparing a great banquet and invited many guests. At the time of the banquet he sent his servant to tell those who had been invited, 'Come, for everything is now ready.' "But they all alike began to make excuses. The first said, 'I have just bought a field, and I must go and see it. Please excuse me.' "Another said, 'I have just bought five yoke of oxen, and I'm on my way to try them out. Please excuse me.' "Still another said, 'I just got married, so I can't come.' "The servant came back and reported this to his master. Then the owner of the house became angry and ordered his servant, 'Go out quickly into the streets and alleys of the town and bring in the poor, the crippled, the blind and the lame.' "'Sir,' the servant said, 'what you ordered has been done, but there is still room.' "Then the master told his servant, 'Go out to the roads and country lanes and compel them to come in, so that my house will be full. I tell you, not one of those who were invited will get a taste of my banquet.'"

Lesson:

Battles are inevitable but so are banquets. Every test and trial brings us closer to him, gives us victory and great authority over our enemy.

Day 7: Reconciled to Love

Do you remember your first crush or your first true love?
How you could not wait to their voice, or talk all night?

Receiving salvation can be just like that, however, over time you may
lose focus or stray from the relationship or begin focusing on yourself.

Rev 2:2-5 (NKJV):
"I know your works, your labor, your patience, and that you cannot bear those who are evil. And you have tested those who say they are apostles and are not, and have found them liars; and you have persevered and have patience, and have labored for My name's sake and have not become weary. Nevertheless I have this against you, that you have left your first love. Remember therefore from where you have fallen; repent and do the first works, or else I will come to you quickly and remove your lampstand from its place—unless you repent.

So how do we get back to our first love? *James 1:1-27 (NASB)*: *Testing Your Faith*

"*James, a bond-servant of God and of the Lord Jesus Christ, To the twelve tribes who are dispersed abroad: Greetings. Consider it all joy, my brethren, when you encounter various trials, knowing that the testing of your faith produces endurance. And let endurance have its perfect result, so that you may be perfect and complete, lacking in nothing. But if any of you lacks wisdom, let him ask of God, who gives to all generously and without reproach, and it will be given to him. But he must ask in faith without any doubting, for the one who doubts is like the surf of the sea, driven and tossed by the wind. For that man ought not to expect that he will receive anything from the Lord, being a double-minded man, unstable in all his ways. But the brother of humble circumstances is to glory in his high position; and the rich man is to glory in his humiliation, because like flowering grass he will pass away. For the sun rises with a scorching wind and withers the grass; and its flower falls off and the beauty of its appearance is destroyed; so too the rich man in the midst of his pursuits will fade away. Blessed is a man who perseveres under trial; for once he has been approved, he will receive the crown of life which the Lord has promised to those who love Him. Let no one say when he is tempted, "I am being tempted by God"; for God cannot be tempted by evil, and He Himself does not tempt anyone. But each one is tempted when he is carried away and enticed by his own lust. Then when lust has conceived, it gives birth to sin; and when sin is accomplished, it brings forth death. Do not be deceived, my beloved brethren. Every good thing given and every perfect gift is from above, coming down from the Father of lights, with whom there is no variation or shifting shadow. In the exercise of His will He brought us forth by the word of truth, so that we would be a kind of first fruits among His creatures. This you know, my beloved brethren. But everyone must be quick to hear, slow to speak and slow to anger; for the anger of man does not achieve the righteousness of God. Therefore, putting aside all filthiness and all that remains of wickedness, in humility receive the word implanted, which is able to save your souls. But prove yourselves doers of the word, and not merely hearers who delude themselves. For if anyone is a hearer of the word and not a doer, he is like a man who looks at his natural face in a mirror; for once he has looked at himself and gone away, he has immediately forgotten what kind of person he was. But one who looks intently at the perfect law, the law of liberty, and abides by it, not having become a forgetful hearer but an effectual doer, this man will be blessed in what he does. If anyone thinks himself to be religious, and yet does not bridle his tongue but deceives his own heart, this man's religion is worthless. Pure and undefiled religion in the sight of our God and Father is this: to visit orphans and widows in their distress, and to keep oneself unstained by the world."*

Scripture Meditation: Mt 6

Lesson: Keep God as your first love. Seek Him first in all things

Day 8: A Proverbs Wife

Written by: Pastor Wendy D.   01/10/1999

Is a woman fit for a King?

Proverbs 31 is God's instructions for a woman to be all that he intended for her to be as well as to receive all her blessings. We as women have and hold the power to create the atmosphere of Love in the home where blessings can abide.

Webster Dictionary defines *'phenomenal'* like this:

"Be unusual in a way that is very impressive."

To be a phenomenal woman means to be a virtuous woman, set apart for the King. Let's breakdown Prov 31:10-31 - Description of a Worthy Woman

"An excellent woman [one who is spiritual, capable, intelligent, and virtuous], who is he who can find her? {A Man who finds a wife, finds a treasure, and He receives favor from the Lord. Prov.18:22}
Her value is more precious than jewels and her worth is far above rubies or pearls.
The heart of her husband trusts in her [with secure confidence],
And he will have no lack of gain.
She comforts, encourages, and does him only good and not evil
All the days of her life. {"Life and death are in the power of the tongue." Pv 18:21}
She looks for wool and flax
And works with willing hands in delight.
She is like the merchant ships [abounding with treasure];
She brings her [household's] food from far away. {enterprising, cultured, prepared by God in advance Eph2:10}
She rises also while it is still night
And gives food to her household
And assigns tasks to her maids.
{prays, intercedes for her family in advance]
She considers a field before she buys or accepts it [expanding her business prudently];
With her profits she plants fruitful vines in her vineyard. {ministry}
She equips herself with strength [spiritual, mental, and physical fitness for her God-given task] And makes her arms strong.
She sees that her gain is good;
Her lamp does not go out, but it burns continually through the night [she is prepared for whatever lies ahead and stays in her word and open to hear God's voice]
She stretches out her hands to the I.e. the staff that holds the textile fibers for spinning distaff,
And her hands hold the spindle [as she spins wool into thread for clothing].
She opens and extends her hand to the poor,
And she reaches out her filled hands to the needy. {"Make level paths for your feet", so that the lame may not be disabled, but rather healed. Heb 12:13}
She does not fear the snow for her household,
For all in her household are clothed in [expensive] scarlet. {covered by the blood of the

46

lamb}
She makes for herself coverlets, cushions, and rugs of tapestry. {anointed}
Her clothing is linen, pure and fine, and purple. {A royal priesthood, a chosen generation... 1 Ptr 2:9}
Her husband is known in the [city's] gates,
When he sits among the elders of the land.
She makes [fine] linen garments and sells them;
And supplies sashes to the merchants. {banners of Love}
Strength and dignity are her clothing and her position is strong and secure;
And she smiles at the future [knowing that she and her family are prepared].
{"Trust in the Lord with all her heart" Pv.3:5-6}
She opens her mouth in [skillful and godly] wisdom,
And the teaching of kindness is on her tongue [giving counsel and instruction].
27 She looks well to how things go in her household,
And does not eat the bread of idleness.
{does not sit around letting her thoughts wonder}
28 Her children rise up and call her blessed (happy, prosperous, to be admired);
Her husband also, and he praises her, saying,
"Many daughters have done nobly, and well [with the strength of character that is steadfast in goodness], but you excel them all."

The source of this remarkable woman's success and competence is revealed in v 30, and it is a source available to everyone. She is wise because she understands and puts into practice the message contained in verse 9 and 10:

"Charm and grace are deceptive, and [superficial] beauty is vain,
But a woman who fears the Lord [reverently worshiping, obeying, serving, and trusting Him with awe-filled respect], she shall be praised.
Give her of the product of her hands, And let her own works praise her in the gates [of the city].

Scripture Meditation: Prv 31

Lesson: Being a true woman, whole and complete:

1. Breaks away from a victim mentality
2. Finds strength in her wisdom not her looks
3. Keeps herself pure in thoughts words and deeds
4. Encourages and strengthens the home and body of Christ, creates healing in her heart and actions.
5. Helps raise the next generation of woman
6. Does not try to take the place of the man, or is bitter towards them, she takes her rightful place and supports him.

Day 9: My Husband, My King...

Written by: Wendy Darline   11/08/2008

(This was the beginning of my new journey, and oh what an amazing journey it's been. One full of tears, laughter, sorrow, pain, and yet, healing and enlightenment.)... So now I share this with you....

One crisp November's day morning, I arose from my bed still healing from the health issues from yesteryear. I finished my morning Bible reading, but I wasn't finished. Something in my spirit was stirring. So I asked of the Lord,

Me: "What is this we are going through together right now?
HIM: "You are not receiving my love."

49

Me: "What?? How am I not receiving your love?" I know your will. I am obedient. I heed to your every call, without hesitation. I interceded for your people and sing praises to your name."

HIM: "Yes, go on."

Me: "I feel your love, power and strength. I know you intimately as my King, my savior, my father, my healer. I have sat at your banquet table and entered your courts with praise. I love to sit under your wings, under the shadow of the Almighty. I sit at the throne room of grace and meditate on your word night and day.

HIM: "Deeper."

Me: "I have always asked for my needs and you have answered my every prayer. I always give you glory and honor for all that you do for me. So how do I not receive your love?

HIM: "Go deeper."

Me: "I have witnessed your signs and wonders. I have allowed you to bring restoration to my past, my relationships, even my finances. I have received homes, cars, jobs and other tangible blessings; I have even received spiritual gifts, territory, and authority; and most of all, I've received supernatural blessings and healings. I have grown up in you and enjoyed your peace, joy and mercy. So how do I not receive your love?"

HIM: "Go deeper."

Me: "I have allowed my identity to be transformed in you and allowed restoration and healing to my flesh, spirit and my soul through your blood. So please talk to me how have I not received your love?"

He sighed.

Me: "My heart is heavy, King; I don't want you mourning a lost loved unnecessarily. I am willing to change to be transformed again and again. I love you so much."

HIM: All of that is true. You are and have done all that and more for me. But –

Me: Yes, Lord, speak to me. I'm listening.

HIM: You don't desire me as your husband. You don't ask me for the desires of your heart. Why don't you trust me to be your husband, to take care of you, to provide for you, to give you gifts beyond your wildest dreams? I put those dreams in you. I am so in love with you,

50

and yet, I can't reach you in that sacred place.
Me: What place is that, my Lord?
HIM: Your inner garden, your bed chamber. I stand at the door and knock covered in dew hoping to hear your thoughts and to give you that one desire of your heart. I want my glance to ravish your heart the way yours has done for me. I want to be that love and rest. The true King of your heart.
Me: The desires of my heart? What are you talking about? I love you, please talk to me. What have I done?

My heart began to sink. Tears seared paths down my cheeks. He has never been mad at me. I've never heard Him be harsh with me. No, I wasn't perfect, but we could talk. He always corrected me gently. He'd convict me and I would acknowledge my misstep and press on. When did this disconnect happen? Or was it even a disconnect? Maybe this is a new season? I wasn't sure so I just kept pressing him for more revelation, more wisdom. I began to pray. For the next several hours, I painstakingly sat there hurting, knowing and feeling the heaviness in His heart. I was so aware of not only His presence, but His burdened heart toward me. I need to fix this and fast. I love him so much. I spent my whole life trying to find him, discover him, know him, relate to him, and now serve him. I can't stay in this place; I had to press through. I began to worship Him, to praise Him, to remind Him of His word and His promises. All of sudden, a soft gentle breeze, more like warm, balmy breath passed over my cheek and neck. He was right next to me ready to reveal His heart to me.

Me: My heart's desire?

I began to think back through my life. Was there something I wanted that maybe I suppressed? All I ever wanted to be is a wife and a mother. I was both-maybe not like I wanted, but I did have a form of it. Nothing else is coming to my mind. My life has been good, great even. I wish my marriage had been one of true love and not of

51

convenience, but that was the only thing I could think of that was still a desire for me... Well, I wanted more children, but I had come to terms after my hysterectomy that I would just have the one--and what an amazing one he is.

HIM: *"Go deeper."*
Me: I desired a relationship with you. To have restoration of my emotions, my past and my present and you gave it to me.
HIM: "Go Deeper."
Me: Okay. To know Your will for my life and my purpose here on Earth. And to have and feel Your love. You've given all of that to me.
HIM: "Go deeper."
Me: "To be loved."
HIM: "Deeper still."
Me: "To be loved as me, the woman.
He exhales somberly.

His sorrow is crushing me. I wish He would just solve this for me quickly so we could move on. But by the way He's taking me, I know that it's going to be heart-wrenching and hard to hear. So I stilled my spirit, bracing for the answer.

HIM: "My daughter. My precious, precious daughter, I have the ability to bring light out of the darkness, to call forth your destiny without the body of Christ. I have used you in ministry and even ordained you to be about my business for the kingdom, which you have done without hesitation. You have been mocked in my name and judged by my people, yet your heart never turned away from me. I even helped you with your enemies. I don't doubt your will or obedience yet...
Me: "Wait, what? What am I not doing? I need you to talk to me. I need you to tell me what I am not doing to cause you this much sadness? Please, I plead.

Now I'm panicking, overcome with emotion, waiting for him to tell me so I can make it better.

HIM: "Go Deeper."
Me: "So this is about me? Me being loved by the Body? Me wanting to be accepted or valued?"
HIM: Not the body, but somebody.
I physically got sick to my stomach like a bad case of the flu.

Me: "Oh god, no. No, I don't want to go through this door. I shut this door. It hurts. Please-please, I'm begging you, don't make me open this one. God, no."
HIM: Yes, this door. I want to give you a man who will love you and see your worth. I want to give you those other children you longed for for years and did not get. I want to bless you and honor you as a bride. My Bride and My Queen. No more warfare, but truly blessed, ruling the kingdom and resting in peace and love and having your hearts desires.
"No!," I said,
God said, "Breathe."

I couldn't. The feelings were raw and unbearable.

Me: "I stuffed those dreams away, filed them under selfishness. When I had my hysterectomy, my then husband did not and would not adopt any children. I was already married, so I was trying to just make that relationship tolerable. But he left. I was wiped out financially, physically, and my son was an adult now. Why do we need to go here?"
HIM: "Because I am not only your God and your King, I am your husband. I want to love on you, adore you and give you these things. I need you to have expectations. Don't you trust me to give them to you? How little you must think of me that you would stuff these away thinking I couldn't fulfill them."
Me: "No, I do, I really do want those things. I really do trust you for those things. But what about free will?"
HIM: "If you will go on this journey with me, I will present you, renew you and bless you."
Me: "How?"
HIM: "First, let the body of believers receive you and then leave it all to me."

He then told me to go to my word and read Revelations 2:4b:

"Nevertheless I have this against you, that you have left your first love..."

Me: I have left my first Love?!

I just sat there in a heap crying for what seemed like an eternity. When I was all cried out, I just shook my head and whispered, "Okay." I never was the girl who fit in at church. I had a loveless marriage and was now divorced, infertile and close to 40. I just surrendered out of exhaustion just thinking of the work ahead, but knowing he was happy. I collapsed and fell asleep. I knew I was about to go to a place where I had to be my most vulnerable in order for God to be this incredible Husband to me.

He reminded me of all I went through the previous year with my health, about almost dying during my surgery and ascending to heaven where he told me he was well pleased and I could come home. He reminded me of when he wanted to know if I would be willing to come back to Earth so He could bless me. I had no idea when I said 'yes,' I would awaken to find my health worse and my old life turned upside down. And now He wants to start all over: a new life, a new Man, a new family. I have no idea how to pray for something like this, so I just whispered, "Okay, God, I trust you. I will receive."

Scripture Meditation: Ps 25

Lesson:
When God brings you His provision, don't question it. Just say "Yes" and "Amen." It will save you a few trips around the mountain.

Day 10: The Dream in His Garden

Written By Wendy Darline, 1997

I lay down to sleep. So much is happening to me. My head is spinning, what is going to happen next? All of sudden I felt a cool breeze come over me. And next thing I know, I am in a garden. It has a stream, flowers everywhere, trees, and to the left, a bench. I hear a soft voice say, "Come sit." So I sat on the bench and looked down realizing my hair had grown long and curlier. My feet were so clean, my dress so pale, no, it was white. I felt alive, beautiful. I felt like I was a teen: renewed, restored and whole. I closed my eyes and listened to the sounds around me. Birds singing, the wind blowing, and the water cascading down in the distance. "Where am I?," was playing over and

55

over in my mind. I began to sing and my heart was full of expectation. I felt someone come up behind me. I knew it was him, My Husband. I began to feel his love and his hands on my head, then an aroma. He was combing and planting flowers in my hair, like he was dressing me as a bride for a wedding. Then he stood in front of me, took me by the hands and said, "Can I have this dance?," he asked. "Yes, I said, "oh yes." So we danced. This was the beginning of my journey with My Husband. Never before had I been in this secret garden. I immediately began writing this down asking God for more, feeling myself forever changed in a good way. It was a new kind of love, a new level of intimacy than ever before.

Scripture Meditation: Deut 8
Lesson:
Intimacy with God is the ultimate goal of every living person.

Day 11: The Mirror

Written By Wendy Darline, 1994

Gen 1:7: "So God made the vault and separated the water under the vault from the water above it. And it was so."

I know the pain of discovery has begun. I feel a transformation coming. So much so that I know I'm going to have to change my thinking in order for this new love relationship to really take off and be all that he intends for it to be. I feel like a caterpillar inside the cocoon. The tearing down process has begun. I wish I could take a look inside myself to see if after all these years I have a solid foundation, or was I just going through the motions. God, all this time was I just existing?? Was all that work and striving done in vain?

"No," I hear him say.

A wave of calm comes over me.

"Is this is just another season in my life?"
"No, this is a caterpillar metamorphosing into a beautiful butterfly.
But first the tearing down, then the recreation, then the pushing
through the cocoon so that your wings will be strong enough to fly."
I sighed, "God I need you."

I have come to know his peace in a new way. I find joy in the struggles
and a level of tranquility that comes from merely speaking his name
and adoring him with songs. These are the gems I carry into this
season. My treasures are worth far more than gold or silver or even
money. This is who I am, my state of being. This life has never been
mine. The moment I got revelation on that was the beginning of my
surrender. No regrets either. I gladly gave it up to the one I love, my
first Love.

He is the breath of my being enveloped in Love, caressed by His
Spirit and mesmerized by his majestic nobility. The roar of his passion
and the touch of his love are mine. He makes me feel complete, whole.

He whispers to me, "You ravish my heart with your glance."

My emotions run high with anticipation of His love. It stirs me. He
stirs me. The seal upon my heart is love and the scar upon his palm
says I am his and he is mine. I am trapped in the fragrance of his
essence and the aroma of his life transcends me. We're together as
one. He sees me. The memories of the dream keep me holding on
today and longing for more to come tomorrow. I hope in Him, trusting
in him to complete this which he has turned on and stirred up. He
knows me; he really knows me. He knows my inner most secrets and
all my flaws, and still he pursues me and loves me dear. He heals me,
transforms me and allows me to come to him flaws and all.

Can my eyes ever see or my ears ever hear what I have so longed
for? I know this is my husband and a spirit. How Lord will you ever be

able to find the one in the natural, the man that will see what you see and still love me? I have longed for the supernatural and the natural to join, yet they always seem to run parallel. Can they really intertwine? Is there really a man on this earth who can really love me? I mean really love me the way you do, and will he Love you the way I do? Can our lives collide and explode with the same level of passion, commitment to create a union, a perfect union? I want it to be like biting into the seed of a pomegranate bursting with flavor and juicy, bitter, yet sweet all at the same time. A pure delight. Oh how my love bursts forth for you. I love you so much. Please protect me from any wolves in sheep's clothing and do not stir this up inside me before it is time.

I began to sing and to focus once again on you, singing *"Come, come away with me, come away with me. Oh how I seek you, I long for you, I miss you."*...Hmm. My beautiful king, there you are, my beautiful king. My Prince of Peace, My Healer, My Redeemer. You are my husband, the lover of my soul. You take my breath away; you make every fear leave. Now I am okay. Take me back to the secret place, to the garden where I first felt this embrace. I'm waiting, hoping, full of excitement. I so treasure our time. I wish we could stay there in that place eternally, in the place where I saw your face. It's like nectar and thick honey so sweet and ripe of past, pure love.

Throughout the bible, God gives us women we can relate to, love and even admire. But most importantly, they are women we can learn from. As I mentioned in the introduction about the steps of the relationships with God, surrendering is shown to us through the Woman at the Well,

"Go and sin no more." Jn 8:11

-- The servant is shown to us by Martha in the story of Martha and Mary. *Lk 10:38-42*
-- The warrior is shown to us in Deborah, *Judges 4*

-- The Bride is clear from Song of Solomon, Ruth and Proverbs 31.
-- The Queen is very real in the book of Esther.

The Bible is full of books that show us relationally how to transform from one relationship with God to another. In this book I will reference the scriptures and books that gave me revelation to what I was hearing from God. Let's stop here and have you read the books God gave me to study during this process of transitioning from surrendered, to servant, to warrior, to a bride and then to the Queen:

Surrender is about letting go.
Servant is about being broken and transformed.
Warrior is learning how to put on your armor and warning against powers and principalities
The Bride is about learning to take your rightful place, tenderness, true love
The Queen now effortlessly knows her worth, loves her king and can take dominion from a place of wisdom and perfect peace.

The tragedy is most of us get stuck between a servant and a warrior and never make room for the King the ministry God has for us. I pray in learning about these women regardless of where you are in the process you will get healing, learn to trust yourself and love yourself others and you will be well on your way to becoming a Queen.

Scripture Meditation:

1 Ptr 4:8:
"Above all, love each other deeply, because love covers over a multitude of sins."

Rom 5:8:
"But God demonstrates his own love for us in this:

While we were still sinners, Christ died for us."

Col 3:14:
"And over all these virtues put on love, which binds them all together in perfect unity."

Lesson:
God created us in His image. We are more than just women and mothers, we are also servants, queens, warriors, and brides to our Father in heaven. We are His children

Day 12: Book of Esther

A woman who was orphaned and adopted and given a new name. longed for a better life, yet was obedient to her caregiver and her religion. She was taken off course, captured and brought to an unknown place where her very heritage yes inheritance was a threat alone to her staying alive, not to mention her becoming the future Queen. So her focus was on her helping her King, seeing herself through his eyes, allowing herself to go through his beauty treatments, his beliefs and seeing his needs and meeting them. Her focus was on her strengths not on her weakness. Also she took chances she prayed often and spoke little, all while keeping her heart compassionate, tender and full of grace.

Esther did not seek the King with her beauty but received wise counsel from both her Father (Uncle) and the King's Eunuch. She waited for her King to call for her. She kept her King safe and kept the enemy at bay. Esther protected Him, his land and the people. She sought counsel, prayed, fasted and then she waited, and then despite her own ridicule and frustration she prepared a banquet for the very enemy trying to kill her and her people.

So you may have read this book in the bible before, however this time read it as a love story with God as the king and Ruth/Queen Vashti being the brides.

Scripture Meditation:
Read Book of Esther as a love story with God as the king and Ruth/Queen Vashti being the brides.

Which bride are you?
Do you come when God calls? If not, what held you back?
Do you go to God before you make decisions?
Do you choose what's best for just you, or what benefits all?

Lesson:
Make Room for the King:
1. Know your place
2. Trust the process
3. Allow God to be your vengeance
4. Stay tender, vulnerable by laying down your sword and picking up your scepter.

Revelation:
As a woman I was never created to be just a warrior, to constantly be in battle. I was to arrive at the palace, lay down my sword and pick up my scepter, to fall in love with my King. Love and Honor are my new levels of authority.

Day 13: Book of Ruth

Ruth is widowed and homeless with no future. Only thing she could do is be released from her mother-in-law and return to her home town. But, instead she takes a leap of faith. She goes home with her mother-in-law to a strange land. She goes to work. She allows herself to be humbled, teachable and sought after. Eventually pursued by Boaz a man of great wealth, yet a man of honor, and abiding by the rules of his land. Goes to town to speak with Naomi's family to see if the Man who should have right to her wants her or wants to relinquish his position to him. He takes Ruth, makes her a bride, gives her a son that she then gives to her mother-in-law Naomi. (She's a foreigner, widowed, but she believed in her mother-in-law's God and trusted the process. Not only was the marriage a blessing to Ruth it brought reconciliation to Naomi's family and honor to Boaz's inheritance and bloodline. But only after she waited! She was a virtuous woman who did not let her eyes wander nor did she let young men cause her to stumble. She kept her eyes on her Lord, and allowed him to be her refuge, and put her trust in him.

These women have been through so many ups and downs, dealing with so much loss. Naomi was bitter and hurting she lost her sons and husbands. Ruth chose better then bitter and decided to follow Naomi to new land, serving God, laboring and walking by complete faith. She obeyed both Naomi and God and so her better trickled over to Naomi and changed Naomi's bitter to better as well as her own.

Scripture Meditation:
Read the *Book of Ruth* as a love story.

> Do you trust God with you loss?
> Do you trust God to take your act of faith a multiply it?
> Do you believe for the impossible?
> God promises to restore. How can you trust God to take away your bitter and give you better?

Lesson:
Walk in Love and Servanthood
1. Seek and follow wise counsel, honor those above you.
2. Walk by faith not by sight.
3. Be patient God is the God of order, allow the man to pursue and get approval. He knows the beginning to the end.
4. Keep from bitterness
5. Do not allow your current circumstances define you and dictate your future.
6. Focus on Reconciliation.

Day 14: Book of Song of Solomon

My favorite, it's our love story. It shows how much our King pursues us, desires us and is captivated by us. It shows me my worth, my beauty, my heart towards the one who desired me first. It exposes the raw emotions of true love, the overcoming of obstacles and wrong thinking, it even shows us how to deal with the naysayers and mockers of this world. The woman was a field worker, a servant mistreated by her family. She did not see herself worthy of the love of a king. She tried so hard to resist him, but ultimately was made just for him and loved him so much. The Shulamite woman is the beloved one. Drifting in and out of the concept of marriage, sees the challenges yet seeks for openness, growth and the joy of this relationship as it unfolds. Still conscious of her flaws, she tries to see herself through her lover's eyes who uses words to entice her, transform her and reaffirm to her that he is someone different. That he can see the woman within.

There is hope of a covenant love that can not and will not be dictated nor defined by the naysayers, the religious ones or the challenges of their differences of this world. They are alike in the spirit and they are entrenched by their convictions for themselves and each other that they can overcome the rest. Hmm... (As much as I am pursuing, I am being pursued), this is altogether new for me.

Lesson:
Intimacy is of God

Chapter 1: *You are lovely*
vs. 2-4 desired to be consumed by him, desires to be one.
vs. 5-7 but when she takes her eyes off him, she focuses on her flaws and starts to self-sabotage this relationship with fear and doubt, clothed as concern of being misled or misunderstood.
vs. 9-11 He validates her by telling her she's lovely, my bride, my queen. She's valuable to him.
vs. 12-14 priceless, precious to her.

Chapter 2: *You are unique and set apart*
She sees herself as one in a bunch. He sees her as separate, one, unique, His. With him she feels safe, loved, fed. "Whole" solely loved - wanted. She has safety, breakthrough, blessings and the victory.

vs. 14-15 Singing destroys the enemies work, it cancels out those who have tried to strip you of your calling or anointing, falsely accused.
vs. 16-17 this draws he4r back to him she wants to feel him near.

Chapter 3: *Patience*

She is looking for him she doesn't feel his presence so she presses in.
She seeks him until she finds him. Keep seeking him, be still and wait,
(don't rush in worship or with your time with him, but stay, sit, wait
for him) the Glory behind the veil.

Chapter 4

vs 9-14 Assurance of a oneness as partnership that God holds me
dearly and is well pleased with me. Honors our relationship as being
an equal partnership. He longs to spend time with me. He looks for it,
longs for that quality time of fellowship and intimacy. 9. good or bad
times you still choose me and that ravishes his heart. One link of the
neck, obedience to divine precepts. Her heart is yielded to do his will.
vs. 12-16 - Speaks to the brides maturity:
a. Garden pleasure solitude and rest to him.
b. Enclosed
c. Kept herself watchful of her heart.
d. His protector.
e. Spring = not polluted by the world
f. Spices-All *note the chief spices represent: *pomegranates* = Broken,
sweet, juicy healing. *Spikenard* = Grace in her ministry, humility.
Myrrh = death of self.
g. Streams of Lebanon = always full, always flowing,
h. Suffering servant.

Chapter 5

vs. 7-8 - She is recognizing her calling. Knowing the heart of God
doubts she can do it, wonders how? Then she surrenders and begins
walking in it, however she becomes criticized by the church because it
doesn't fit into the religious box. She leaves the church but continues

to seek his face.

vs. 9 - The church is questioning her and her intentions. Judgmental.

vs. 10 - she does not waiver. she tries to show them what she sees what she feels she tries to show them his glory.

Chapter 6

vs. 1 - the church decides it wants to pursue this glory as well.

vs. 2-3 - confirms that commitment the covenant relationship.

My First Revelation: *He does really turn ashes into beauty:*

As I forgive and release others in my life, I begin to see the process lifting from grief into enlightenment. I forgave the husband, the abandonment, the forsaken heart, the empty promises, the broken covenant, bitterness, rejection, and myself... I am having an awakening come over me to the extent of our makers love. My heart is drawing closer to him. I want more; I want to go deeper and know his heart, his secrets and have his fresh revelation in my life. I feel pursued as well; this passion inside me is new. For so long I was afraid of intimacy because of rejection, but this, this is a different type of love where only He and I can abide.

Scripture Meditation:

Read Song of Solomon as a love story between you and Jesus.

Do you hesitate to come when He calls?

Do you feel you are unlovely or unlovable?

Do you know Jesus as your bridegroom who loves you and sees your infinite beauty?

Day 15: Liquid Love

A Poem by Wendy Darline, 1989

Holy, holy, holy
Resting in his glory
Holy, Holy, Holy is his majesty
Baptized anew, refreshed and so free
I become weak, and He is made strong
It is a brand new day, I hear a new song
My King your grace and tenderness is merciful to me
You won't relent until you have it all, my heart, mind, soul, true liberty
You have set me on fire, water can't quench this fire is inside of me
I'm learning how to breathe and to receive thee
This love is new and free like liquid, liquid love that is taking over
inside of me.

Scripture Meditation: Jer 20

Lesson:

Put on soaking music and reread the scriptures, pray this prayer:

Father God, I ask for creativity to be released through me and your Holy Spirit. Fill this place with more of you, Amen

Now take pen to paper, or hand to clay, or paint brush to canvas and listen for him to give you your own song, poem or vision,

Day 16: His Touch

Written by: Wendy Darline 2/14/1996

How is this even possible? This late in life? This late in the game... that he should come? The way he holds my hand to pray makes me feel connected. The firmness of his hand as it leads the small of my back and lets me know he's in charge and leading me where we need to go. I feel protected, safe and alive all at the same time. The gentle way he brushes his hand across my cheek and then into my hair lets me know he wants to kiss me, that he desires me. The outstretched arm and hand held tight lets me know he is my one, my only. It shows we are together trudging forward hand and hand against the world supporting one another.

The way he takes me in his arms and holds me tight makes my stomach do flips, all the while making my body hot and longing for more of him. His hot breath on my neck as he lingers gently kissing the nape of my neck and pulling me into him tighter deeper and more intensely shows me there can and will never be anyone else for him or I. Our desire, our want and our need for one another starts off gently, tenderly, kind of spiritual and innocent. Then in an instance, it turns almost animalistic, uncontrollable and more ravenous than can be explained. Each push, pull, stroke, kiss and touch just increases the desire for one another. It's bringing all healing of hurts, disappointments and voids back into perspective that nothing and nobody means as much as this right here.

Right in this moment the entire reason for being is transformed into a new language that only we can receive and interpret for one another. I feel alive, young and restored. I can't remember any of what was bothering me. This is the brief time in space where time actually doesn't exist and I come completely out of my head, allowing my soul, my heart and my body to become one in total agreement. To the point that my body explodes with total ecstasy. To have and to be had by this Man. I feel safe, secure and totally wanted.

Never before have I felt so alive, so mindful of my emotions, my passions and my hopes. My heart beats with his, my soul connects to his as we lay spent and breathless. The way he entangles his body in mine and holds me lets me know I'm all his and not just what he desired for the moment, but what he chooses for LIFE! My whole life I waited for the perfect moment, the perfect kiss, the perfect touch that would explain to me why we long for Love. Why we desire one another for companionship despite the heartaches and all the disappointments. The answer. So that at the end of our life, we'd be able to stand in his presence and say, "It all was worth it."

My moment is now; my moment is here. It's in the way he laughs, the way he talks, the way he looks at me, but most of all, it's in his touch...

Scripture Meditation: Gen 2:24, Mt 19:5, Mk 10:8

Lesson:
God desire was always for us to have a partner, to become one with another is God's plan for wholeness and strengthened companionship.

If you're married, you must look at intimacy as a way of refreshing one another and ministering to your spouse. It also refreshes the other half of you. So make sure you are not bringing problems into your bed, but really see it as a time of communion and healing for your spouse. Do not withhold intimacy from your spouse because this allows strife and illness to have an open door in your marriage and cause a tear (foothold) like rejection, distrust, and spiritual attacks to slip into your marriage.

For those that are single, you are whole and complete. And best of all, your intimacy comes from Christ. Don't allow another to come into that space until they are your spouse, because they will be taking away from you, not adding to you. Your oil is precious and needed for refreshing, so as you abstain you have the reassurance from God that He will give you water that will cause you to never thirst again

Day 17: Extravagant Worship

Written By Wendy Darline, For The Choir, 1994

As I lay resting and soaking in his presence, I hear him whisper,

"Sing to me. Pursue me. Tell me how much you love me and come to me so I can share my heart with you."

I feel him next to me. I begin to sing to him, to tell him how much I love him and desire him. His heart was heavy; he began to weep, and I continued to sing. I saw angels come into the room and sing as well. It was so lovely and harmonious. My heart ached for my King. He longed to be pursued and his heart was truly being lifted as we poured song after song into the atmosphere. Healing began to arise. The songs of recognition, of praise, and of gladness permeated the atmosphere. Love, grace, hope, and most of all, the glory arose. Laughter took over and he was whole again.

God is the lover of us. He is the creator who made us in his image as a companion, a mistress, and a lover. God truly is our bridegroom and enjoys loving us, courting us and pursuing us. However, he loves it as well. He desires our love, worship, thankfulness and most of all, us, completely abandoned in and for him. Over time, love, intimacy and passion have been torn down by the church. It has been made to feel cheapened and wrong-unless between a husband and a wife-and strictly for the purpose of procreation. The world has turned it into something self-fulfilling and non-essential in forms of covenant and or perspective of another human being and their needs and wants. Both have made it very unappealing.

True intimacy and fulfillment comes when you are wholeheartedly entangled together for the sheer purpose of celebrating each other, abandoning ourselves for the other with gratitude, and a desire to feel connection of both mind and body. A heart that is happy and a soul that is satisfied will automatically result in a happy and health perspective of this. Including our Maker in this process brings forth order, establishes boundaries that provide safety, and frees the pollution of greed, lust and selfishness that corrupts our minds and hearts. Being completely surrendered allows for the greatest healing, love and compassion to transpire between us, our maker, and others.

Scripture Meditation:

Ps 149:
"Praise the Lord.[a]
Sing to the Lord a new song,
his praise in the assembly of his faithful people.
Let Israel rejoice in their Maker;

let the people of Zion be glad in their King.
Let them praise his name with dancing
and make music to him with timbrel and harp.
For the Lord takes delight in his people;
he crowns the humble with victory.
Let his faithful people rejoice in this honor
and sing for joy on their beds.
May the praise of God be in their mouths
and a double-edged sword in their hands,
to inflict vengeance on the nations
and punishment on the peoples,
to bind their kings with fetters,
their nobles with shackles of iron,
to carry out the sentence written against them—
this is the glory of all his faithful people.
Praise the Lord."

Song of Sol 1:1-3:
"Let him kiss me with the kisses of his mouth-`For your love is better than wine.
Because of the fragrance of your good ointments, Your name is ointment poured forth; ..."

Song of Sol 1:12-14:
"While the King is at his table, My spikenard sends forth its fragrance. A bundle
of myrrh is my beloved to me, That lies all night between my breasts. My beloved is
to me a cluster of henna blooms in the Vineyards of En Gedi."

Lesson:
He too wants to feel loved and pursued, Rev 2:4:

*In both worship and intercessory prayer remember to be still and to listen to the lover of your heart.
*Know he needs and desires you as much as you need him.

*Intimacy is his true hearts desire
*Healing resides where love abounds

Day 18: A Love Story

(Pt. 2)

Written by Wendy Darline - 08/10/1991

Today I awoke soaked in my own sweat and tears, longing to be close to the one who brought me life. I wanted to go into the secret place, the garden where I first fell in love with him as my new husband. I closed my eyes and began to breathe in the very essence of Him, the one I call Husband. As I began singing and filling the air with thankfulness, I felt His sublime warmth and peace as He entered the room. His spirit entangled with mine. I knew we were about to have an amazing encounter once more. Oh, how I love these times with my Husband.

I began to drift into a meditative state, not asleep, but an unbridled bliss of love and heaven all swirled together creating for me a perfect, unrestrained trust that allowed me to let down my guard, my walls, to receive the healing, rest, and completeness He has for me. It transported me from this fleshly life to my supernatural life where I am always whole and complete and loved.

I glide into our garden that lies between our two bed chambers that can only be entered into by coming out of one of the rooms. As I amble toward my bench where I wait for my king, I notice Him already sitting there. Hmm, this is different. I quickened my pace to reach him. As I approached the one I love, He arose, took my hand and escorted me out of the garden through a gate I never knew was there. It was hidden by the bougainvillea that was thick and lush. I'm a little confused; I so wanted time with Him. Where are we going? Why are we leaving our garden?

We gallivant through the lush, verdant foliage, my hand in his, and come into a vast field. In that field, a young girl frolics. Upon closer inspection, I realize that girl is me. I am about 5 years old. Up ahead, I see a young boy running toward me. He is dark, like ebony dark. He gets close to and he's laughing. I begin to giggle, too. He wants to play. My Husband takes my hand and gives it to the boy, who pulls me out into the field. Poppies blossom everywhere as we are playing, twirling, laughing and giggling. We chase butterflies; I chase him; he chases me. He pulls my hair firmly. "Ouch," I exclaimed, as I turned to him with a hurt face.

He's standing there with a sheepish grin and a flower in his hand. I curtsied, took the flower, and we began playing some more. We ran until we collapsed in a heap in the tall grass. As we caught our breath, the sun was shining so radiantly. It feels so nice here. He lies next to me twirling my golden curl around his finger. It looked like gold spun around his dark finger.

He lets go of my hair, stands up and motions for us to go into the water. I'm hesitant for only a minute, but then I jumped right in. The water's so cool and refreshing. We splash each other and laugh like there's not a care in the world. He begins to splash harder in such a way that causes a rolling wave that I got sucked into and pulled under. I'm now submerged in the murky water and can't see my way back up. I begin to panic and then I feel his hands under my armpits lifting me up toward the surface. As our heads jut above the surface, I take a huge breath. He looks into my eyes and sees I'm petrified. He pulls me into him and kisses my forehead ever so softly. A tear falls down my face. I feel reassured in his arms. I'm okay.

We swim to the dock and he pulls me out. As we get out of the water, I notice his arms are a little stronger and have some muscle definition to them. We are no longer little children, but young teens. As I lay next to him, I rest my head on his chest and it's much bigger than before.

He gently cups my chin in his firm hand and peers into my eyes to see if I was okay. I smiled oh so big and then proceeded to pull his face to mine to give him a few butterfly kisses. He took his hand, tousled my hair and smiled. We hardly seem to speak with words, but every once in a while, I feel his heart speak to mine. I know when it happens because my skips a beat every time. When he does speak to me, he whispers in my ear, "Ever after." I blush whenever he says that, not sure what it means exactly.

He wraps his legs around mine and pulls me near for a hug. To me, this is home. Wherever he is, wherever we are, this is how I know I'm home, I'm safe and I am loved. In his arms, I am home. After a little while of listening to his robust heartbeat, I begin to doze off. He wakes me to get up and we begin to run some more. We run and run through the never ending meadow chasing and tagging one another. We take each other by the hands and twirl as fast as we humanly can, creating our own warm summer breeze in this midsummer afternoon. We fall down into the tall grass still laughing at one another and enjoying the presence of each other's company knowing that we are the very best of friends.

We lie in the grass, arm in arm, holding each other, trying to catch our breath. He pulls me into his chest and wraps me in those big, safe arms once more and whispers in my ear, "Ever after." This time I cried a single tear. As it streams down my face, he wipes it away and kisses my forehead, and then my lips. Whoa, he's never done that before. An indescribable feeling surges through my body like a gentle stirring, not really, more like an intense tremble. I become more aware of his strength, his warmth, and even his body. "I'm safe," as I melt into his arms.

As I lay there looking into his hazel brown eyes, I see our Father, our Comforter, looking back at us, reassuring us that He is near. We sigh together, then jump up. He takes me by the hand and we run excitedly towards our Father. We leap right into His arms and he holds us both in a warm embrace. He touches us on the top of our heads and kiss our foreheads. I feel safe. I look at my very best friend. He looks so loved and adored. A tear tumbles down his face. Our Father wipes it with his cloak, I know we are safe. His tear tugs at my heart and opens me up to see him not just as a friend. Something's changed. He is not just a boy anymore. He looks different to me now. Something in my stomach stirs toward him. The words erupt in my mind, I love him.

Our Father twirls us around while speaking words over us that fill the air with a kind of musical harmony that makes you feel alive, refreshed, loved. He is so pleased with His children. We look up into the lucid sky, and my very best friend, my love, points and says, "There!" I look and realize my love is showing me angels in the sky twirling and singing right above us. We look for our Father and he is nowhere to be found, so we continue to watch and listen.

He stretches out his hand to mine. As he pulls me near his face, I notice a stubbly shadow on his face, something new. He no longer looks smooth like a boy, but this on his face, hmm. It feels like hair, but shorter, bumpier. I meld into his body. He is so much stronger now, bigger in every way. I feel small in his arms, but I also feel even safer and more protected than ever. I breathe him in. He even smells different to me. So much change, but yet, peace engulfs me. As we dance, he sings a song, one of love and of acceptance and longing for just me. I nuzzle into the nape of his neck as he leans into my face and whispers into my ear, "Ever after."

I sing softly into his ear now and the angels join in. I feel hungry and thirsty, my body's reaction to his touch, his voice and his warmth. He places one hand on the lower part of my back, the other is entangled in my hair and caressing my head. He kisses me gently on top of my head. His kisses made me feel complete, but something is changing in me. I begin to yearn for more. I feel drawn to him, concerned for him, and now looking for more of a sense of love and approval from him than ever before. My heart's not my own any more, yet I feel strangely calm and at peace with this new thing arising in me. I feel alive. I know that I am loved.

It begins to rain. He grabs me and we run, and run, and run until we breathlessly fall and collapse under a giant tree. He dabs the water from my face ever so sweetly and I wipe the dew drops from his brow. He thanks me, cups my face with his gentle hands, and kisses my face long and hard. He gazes deep into my eyes until all the shivering leaves my body. I am warm again. Wow, he looks so grown and mature. We both do. My hair is past my waist and his beard is now full. I always know the time when we both change because his arms become fuller and muscular. He is my warrior. I know how hard he works by the places on his hands that are rough, no longer are they soft and pliable. His stomach ripples with muscles from laboring. He is so beautiful to me. Dark and oh so lovely next to my pure white skin. He complements mine and I His. I see our Father in him. He pulls me down onto his lap and holds me tight in his arms. He is finding his rest in me. I am feeling my safety in him.

As I run my hands down his arms, I see pictures on his arms. His life's story is permanently embedded in his skin creating a collage of our lives. It shows his past, his pain, his joy, his struggles, his victories, and an homage to those he lost along the way. He reaches into his pocket and pulls out a small piece of fruit and begins to feed me. With each bite I take, he kisses my mouth tenderly. I in turn take the fruit and press it against his lips for him to take a bite. But he, knowing the fruit is too small to share, shakes his head 'no'. As I take another sumptuous bite, he leans into my face and whispers in my ear, "Ever after".

Suddenly, thunder and lightning boom and crackle across the foreboding sky. It's starting to get dark. He takes off his shirt and puts it around my shoulders. I shake my head wondering, how will he stay warm? He winks to me that he's okay. I reach out for his hand, but he starts walking away. Where is he going? I start to follow him, but my Father stops me and says, "I'm here." I search for my love, but I can't see him. It's so dark. My Father says, "He'll be right back." I'm cold. I've never been cold. Why am I cold? What's happening? Something is different in me. I shiver and my Father gently takes his wings and wraps them around me, saying again, "I am here." Those words use to bring me such comfort. Why didn't it make my peace return this time? "He will return soon." I take a breath and try to close my eyes to rest knowing my love will return.

Later, I awaken, startled, realizing I'm still alone. I call for him, Wow, my voice is loud. I've never before had to be speak in more than a whisper. Where does this change come from? I feel a sense of loss, panic even. "Where are you?," I cry out. "Love, where are you?" I hear a voice, but it's not his. It's my Father saying, "I'm here. He'll be right back." I'm crying softly at first, but now a little harder. It's still dark. He's not right back. It seems forever since he held me in his arms. I feel separated, torn, no longer whole. Why, why do I feel this way? I begin to sing, not out of joy, but desperation to feel some type of peace. My Father holds me tighter, his arms and wings wrapping me up into a cocoon till I close my eyes once more and sleep, collapsed. Father, whispers to me, "Trust me." I breathe... He will be right back... I start to dream about him, coming back to me. Remembering him as a child, being my friend, the warmth of the sun, the kisses and hugs, the words he whispered in my ear, "Ever after."

His wings embrace me tighter. I'm safe, yes, but why don't I feel secure? "I do know this, I am loved, "I whisper in a muddled sob. "Father I miss him, I love him. Where oh where did he go? Why did he leave me behind? My heart aches." My father wipes the tears that flood my face and kisses my forehead. "You're okay," He says, "He will be right back. Trust me, he will be right back." I nod in agreement to trust him. I take a deep breath, wipe my and clenching my hands to my heart. I nestle into my Father's chest and fall into a deep sleep. I hear my father's heartbeat. He knows I'm trusting Him for what seems like the impossible. I am trusting Him for what I cannot see.

I no longer hear the rain; instead I feel sun on my face. I wake up and see the sun shining brightly over all of the fields. I search for my love... He's still is not here. My head falls as I speak softly to my Father, "I'm trusting you." "Come with me, my Father says. He leads to the nearby bubbling brook. As we stand near the shore, He scoops water in his hands and says, "Drink." I drink from his hands. The water tastes refreshing and sweet. I want more. I continue to drink from his hands a never ending stream of thirst-quenching water. Then he hands me a piece of fruit, different from that of my love. I shook my head no-I did not want to eat without my love.

Where is he? He didn't eat before he left. What if he needs it? What if he's hurt? I need to go find him. My Father shakes his head no and tells me to take it and eat. He assures me he's fine and will be right back. I take the fruit, say thank you, then tear into it. Juices explode out of it and drips down my hands. As I licked my hands clean, it turned into warm honey. I licked my fingers until I was full. I wished my love was here knowing he would love to taste this as well. I whispered to my Father, "I miss him; I love him. Please bring him back to me."

"Do you trust me really?," my Father asks. I felt a stirring in my belly. I heard a soft voice say "Ever after," then I smiled and said, "Yes, I really trust you." Peace came upon me once more. He points me to a bench near the water and I go and take a seat. He pours water upon my head and begins washing my hair and feet. He gives me a new purple and gold robe to put on. It was so beautiful. I never really paid attention to my clothes before, but there was no mistaking how beautiful this robe was. It was fit for royalty, a queen. He began to place flowers in my hair as angels sang causing my belly to fill with laughter and joy. I found myself giggling and laughing for no real reason. Ribbons flowed from my dress and hair. I thought how unnecessary; I felt silly. The angels shook their heads at me and said, "Not silly, beautiful. Not necessary, but very necessary."

I suddenly was conscious of my body. My breasts were full; my waist tiny. I'm no longer a girl. I am a woman. I am a full-fledged woman. I leaped up and looked in the water to see my reflection. My hair, my face, my lips. I lifted my gown, looking over every part of my flesh. Is this why my love left? Did I change too much? Have I changed to where he no longer will recognize me, he no longer will find me to be his heart's desire?!

I suddenly felt a hand on my back. I turned, and there she was. This beautiful woman, the most beautiful woman I had ever seen. Her eyes blue like the sky and her dress so bright I could see right through her. Her voice was like a song. I looked down at the sash around her neck and it said the word "Comforter." She began to speak to me and tell me that I was beautiful, that I looked just like my Father, and that I was a going to be a queen. She said that my Father had placed everything that my love would ever desire or need in me and that I just need to believe.

I felt a new life inside me. I felt strong and powerful. I felt so loved and so-so beautiful. Confident that I am who my Father says I am. I am who my Comforter says I am. I am confident that I am who the angels says I am. My heart feels alive, I feel so happy and full of joy. I begin to sing. The sky fills with birds. A rainbow arched over us and the angels wept with joy. My Father came to me, his face flooded with tears of joy. I wiped His tears with my sleeve and in my hands, diamonds appeared. I looked at him puzzled and began to giggle. My Father was now looking to me like a King. He grabs me by the hand and we dance. I hadn't danced with Him in a long time. It was a newness that felt strange. It was both happy, and yet, sad all at once. I began to remember my love and dancing with him, missing his touch. I suddenly was conscious of the time. It seemed like forever since I had seen my love. Did he think of me? Did he know where to find me? Would he even want me after all this time had passed? Right then, the wind blew and I heard wafting through the air, "Ever after."

I had peace and began to meander into the field trying to remember his face and what he looked like now. I giggled to myself remembering his goofy smile, his childish antics, and his playful gestures toward me. I felt my love for him return like a flood and fill me to the brim of my heart's capacity. "Father, take care of him for me till he returns." My Father takes me by the hand and says, Come walk just a little bit farther." I simmered with anticipation of where my King was taking me. I didn't recognize where I was at all. This place was lush green marvel. It lots of fully-matured fruit trees, each had their vibrantly-colored fruit to present to the warm sun. Beautiful flowers of all kinds and colors, all in sequence with the promises of my Father much like a rainbow.

Animals were dancing and skipping and playing in the fields. In the distance, I saw a cascading waterfall. I love it here. It's so beautiful, rich and full of life. I went toward the waterfall for a drink, but my Father grabbed my hand and said, "No, not yet." I stood puzzled. He said, "Come just a little bit further." We passed the waterfall and there along the other side of the water was a door. A large wooden door with carvings of roses and a fruit tree carved deep into the mahogany wood.. As I approached it warily, I saw carvings on it. I went to touch it and my Father said, "Wait a minute." I stood in silence, curious and confused. Father placed a few more flowers in my hair, new ones from this land, that were lavender and full of fragrance. He bowed his head and said, "Enter." I knocked. There was no answer. I was sure I was at the home of the beautiful woman that bore the name "Comforter" because her aroma and presence became thick to me. This had to be her place. So I knocked again. Still no answer. My Father giggled and said, "No, turn the knob."

I reached out my hand and turned the knob, and there standing in white garments was a man, his arms stretched out towards me to welcome me. His head was bald. His hands held flowers in one like a huge bouquet and in the other a bottle of wine. I ambled toward the man. When I got close, I hugged him hello. And as I did, he whispered in my ear, "Hi there, Ever After. My Ever After." Huh?? I pulled back and looked the man in the eyes, "It's you!" It's my love." I touched his face. "Please don't let this be a dream," I said as tears flooded my eyes. It's his voice, his eyes. I barely recognize him. He looks older, wiser and so full of love and life. He is big and strong, yet his beard is shorter and it has spots of white in it. He smiles and laughs and hands me the flowers and wine.

As I take them and free his hands, he grabs me and twirls me. It's him: the boy, my friend, and the man I love. The one who knows me and has been with me. He nuzzles his face in my hair like long be,fore and we begin to dance. My love, he really didn't forget me. He still wants me. I feel so happy so loved. He pulls me away for a minute, looks me up and down while taking in all of my changes. He likes them all! He still looks at me with desire, with love.

As my eyes move about the room soaking in every detail, I set the flowers and the wine on a table and I run to him. He picks me up in his big arms and twirls me around like before. He pulls me close and says, "Are you ready?" I looked at him puzzled and then nodded yes. He escorted me to the table, poured wine into a glass, and then took some fruit and pulled it apart. It was marvelously succulent. He put the fruit to my lips! Wait!, his hands were dripping in honey. I licked the honey from his finger and then ate the fruit. I fed him a piece of the fruit, too. As I did, my hand filled with honey as well. He proceeded to eat both the honey from my hand and the fruit, then he kissed my lips hard, pressing my lips to his for a long time. Never ever had he kissed me like this before. My legs became weak and I almost fell, but he caught me and pulled me close. He tore some bread and dipped it into the wine and handed it to me. Then he dipped another piece of bread in the wine. He fed his bread to me and I fed him with mine. Our Father came to the table and said, "It is done," and we both started crying. My love whispered in my ear, "our Ever After."

I took his face in my hands and stared deeply into his eyes until his arms and legs trembled. But this time I caught him before he collapsed. He smiled at me with tears of joy as we held each other for what seemed to be an eternity. I'm home. Angles fill our home, a home he built with his own two hands. They sing songs of praise and joy as we dance and fill each other overflowing with love, embraces and gentle kisses. Soon, our Father calls us to Him. He pulls us into his bosom. His wings wrap around us. We are complete. Our Father cries with joy. He looks us both in our eyes and says, "Thank you for trusting in me."

He tells my love to kneel and places a scepter in my right hand. I gently tap it on his right shoulder, then his left. He's now my king, my lover, my friend, my husband. Our Father takes my left hand and places it on my husband's bowed head and as my husband lifts his head, our Father asks me, "Are you well pleased?" I said, "Yes," then out of my head a crown was formed upon my husband's head and inscribed in it was the word gift. Then our Father tells him to stand.

He rises with a strengthened resolve. Our Father asks, "Do you receive your gift?" My husband says, "Most definitely yes." Then both out Father and my husband place their left hands upon my head and out came a crown and engraved was the word "blessed." Our Father then handed my husband a scroll and placed a signet ring upon my right hand and it was done. Our Father grinned proudly and said, "Now it is complete." My husband and I held hands and oil began to drip from our palms. "Ever After."

Scripture Meditation: Mt 11:28; Song of Sol 2:10; Is 45:3; Ps 91

Lesson:
God's always working out the details. He knows the end from the beginning. That's why He wants our eyes on Him, not on our circumstances or our own expectations. Trusting in Him, frees you from worry or frustration and keeps your heart from becoming sick.

Pray and ask Him if you haven't already to renew your mind, then focus your thoughts and position your heart to be aligned with Him, and watch and see how much freer you feel and become.

Day 19: A Beautiful Landscape

Written by: Pastor Wendy Darline - 07/18/1988

As I lay and reflect back on my earlier years. I think often about the picture He painted for me. I was not yet a glimmer in my parents eyes, not even a perspective. Yet he shared with me. He had a paint palette in one hand and a brush in the other and he began to paint the most amazing picture for me. Careful to include the shading and the background. Assuring me that many times it may be dark or you may not see me yet he said think back on this.

I asked him as he put the blue and the hints of white, what do all

93

these colors represent to me. He said they are part of the landscape, part of the journey along the way. They will be your markers or your signs along the way to remind you that I created you and this, and that I am still with you, it will be your guide as well as a reminder of all my promises. That you have a destiny to complete and that you will have glimpses of memories to help guide you along the way. I was paying close attention to every stroke of the brush as it turned a blank white canvas into a picture, paying close attention to the details it was laying out the map of my life, creating a sense of worth for me. I knew that when I got to earth that I would be filled with joy, revelation, great wisdom, perspective and understanding.

I began to get excited for the journey, for the people I would meet. I love my master and I knew that he always wanted the best for me and that if he created it, it would be beautiful, amazing, and perfect. (At least this was my thought process at the time). Little did I know that with the long journey to get here, that vision would become somewhat dismal, distorted even forgotten at times.

I had no understanding of the Man who had been abolished from his own destiny would begin to try and steal mine. To cause me to doubt experience fear and otherwise question myself and my truth at times. Yes I stumbled, I fell hard at times but I kept on getting up. When I was in his presence and the picture was in front of me it all seemed simple, exciting very relatable. Now I tend to second guess this road or that. I tend to think real hard on things that don't have any relevance towards the goal yet seem so significant at the time.

He is so amazing to me so full of life and hope so encouraging and full of love that I feel I can do anything. Yet here I feel so tangible, so insignificant. The earth is big yet in actuality is very tiny in the big picture. Funny how you go from seeing so clearly to seeing nothing but the obstacles and giants. When in actuality they are really nothing more than stepping stones under your feet. That is when meditation, rest and song comes into play, your need to find strength and get back to your maker and His perception, His wisdom and His grace. So you again can find hope faith peace and the grace to go another day. He showed and shared so much with me that it's hard for me to settle for anything less then everything he gave to me.

Sometimes I just want greater understanding as to how to get the things from up there down here. To help me, aid me, guide me to this place I know I need to get to. And also who to pick up and who to leave along the way. So I pick up the paintbrush in my mind and begin to paint alongside him, filling in the places He's left for me, including my perspective, my talent, it's truly a unique masterpiece of love.

Scripture Meditation:

Ps 139:13-14:
"For tho hast possessed my reins, thou hast covered me in my mothers womb. I will praise thee, for I am fearfully and wonderfully made; marvellous are thy works; and that my soul knoweth right well."

Jer 1:4-5:
"Then the word of the Lord came unto me saying, Before I formed thee in the belly I knew thee; and before thou camest forth out of the womb I sanctified thee, and I ordained thee a prophet unto the nations."

Gal 1: 15:
"But when it pleased the Lord, who separated me from my mother's womb, and called me by his grace, to reveal his Son in me, that I might preach him among the heathen, immediately I conferred not with flesh and blood

Lesson:
This metaphor is to show you the very depths God went to while planning your destiny and the journey for your life. Connecting back to Him is the highest love you will ever find. Connecting back to your Maker and reaching your fullest potential will leave your heart satisfied and determined to continue this fight here on Earth.

Day 20: Water Of My Soul

Written by Wendy Darline, 2017

Today started out like every other day so I supposed. Yet it wasn't, as I started towards the hills where I normally go to gather my thoughts and to worship in his presence. Something kept telling me to go deeper, and as I walked through those hills through the deep lush woods, I began to hear what seemed to me as loud thunder. As I got closer to the sound I discovered a waterfall, the water beating on the pool beneath and the rocks all around it was like a sound of worship from heaven. Crystal blue water and snow white mist. It smelled fresh, new, it was a pool of transformation.

As I approached the water, I felt the urge to just stare at the clear water, but he nudged me. Not physically but gently in my ear, go in let me wash you. So I dove in and swam underneath the waterfall, that lead me into a cave, now the water was a veil, shielding me from the world.

I felt as if I had been here before with Him. My true love, as I sat in this water and soaked, tears ran down my face. Water has always be so healing for me, like liquid love pouring down on me. On another occasion my King came and washed the dirt from my feet. However, I have been sick for a very long time, and wore down from the battles and elements of this world, so sitting in this water not too hot, not too cold; I felt my bruised and battered body responding with relief. He has always looked after me with such care. I remember when my first love had called my name and asked me to take him into my heart. He told me I was washed white as snow, and that he would always satisfy my thirst.

I took my hands and made a cup and scooped up some of the water and began to drink, I was so thirsty. My heart and my soul started to skip a beat and I began to feel the healing power of my true love wash over me.

He whispered in my ear, "Stay here and just soak with me".

I began to sing songs from the book that he had written for me, and to quote its many verses. I submerged myself in the water and allowed not only this healing water wash me but his very presence and his many words to cleanse me, heal me and bring me a strength that surpasses all understanding. He truly is a generous King, a King who pours out his love on me daily, always knowing what I need and wanting to find a way to bring me love, support and comfort after the world has torn me down, and the sins of this world have beaten at my flesh. He never said I would not suffer in this land but he did however say that he would be there to heal me, restore me and to love me through my many battles, trials and storms.

The water he uses to wash me and make me white again, the water he uses to take away my daily thirst, the water is what poured out his side while he hung on a cross for me. My king, he died for me so that I could live this life with him and for him. Together defeating the many enemies, overcoming darkness, setting the captive free and what cost? The cost he was willing to pay on the cross, beaten and bloody for me. There is no battle to great for me, for I know he goes before me and is there with me every step of the way, and when it's done he invites me to the throne room to hear the praises and to worship with him and the saints in glory.

I long to be in his presence and am thankful for these times alone with him. Weather it is at his throne room, a banquet, or the garden it is always a time to be restored and to speak of his heart and the goodness of his grace and mercy. Have you ever felt like this world has taken a toll on you? Then run into your savior's arms dive into your word and allow it to submerge you wash you and quench your thirst. He is waiting.

Scripture Meditation:

Ps 42:7:
"Deep calls to deep at the roar of your waterfalls, all your breakers and your waves have gone over me."

Ps 42:1-2a:
"As a deer pants for flowing streams, so pants my soul for you, Oh God. My soul thirsts for God, for the living God."

Jn 4:14:
"But whoever drinks the water I give them will never thirst. Indeed, the water I give
them will become in them a spring of water welling up to eternal life".

Eph 5:26:
"To make her Holy and clean, washed by the cleansing of God's word."

Ps 51:7 (NKJV)
"Purge me with hyssop, and I shall be clean."

Jn 13:14:
"If I then, your Lord and Teacher, have washed your feet,
you also ought to wash one another's feet."

Lesson:
Trust God cares, turn your cares to Him and soak in His goodness. I love visualizing Him giving me water to drink and caring for my every need. Remember you're no longer your own, so know He is right there going through it all with you. Thank you, God.

Day 21: It Is Finished!

(My Husband, My King Pt. 2)
November 8, 2009

(Excerpts taken from "The Prodigal Couple" book)

I woke up January 1st, 2009. God spoke to me so clearly, "Go to the beach. I want to spend time with you." I was so excited. God wants time with me! So, I got up that morning, grabbed my trusty bible and notebook, and headed to the beach. Looking forward to spending time with Him made me giddy like a schoolgirl as to what we had in store for me today. Never did I think it would be about a *new husband*, a new ministry, and a new life. So soon?!

When I was lying in the hospital bed, God gave me a choice: a) I can go home to be with Him (because I had done my job well) or b) I can go back so that he could give me the one desire of my heart He hadn't fulfilled, which was a husband to love me and do ministry with. *{Note: My husband and I were not saved when we got married. My salvation came the year after, yet, I honored my marriage and him: praying, fasting and believing for his salvation and service with me.}*

I agreed with God to come back. But in light of my circumstances that followed, I felt this new husband prophecy was just a dream. But God. "The new thing." Right? "No longer forsaken," is what God would say to me every morning for the following months.

Is 62:4: "No longer will they call you deserted, or name your land desolate. But you will
be called Hephzibah (The city of Gods delight), and your land Beulah ("The Bride
of God"); for the Lord will take delight in you, and your land will be married.

I began to bawl like a baby in front of my King. I whispered," God you know what they have said; you know how they all feel about me. But God, you see me."

"She gave this name to the Lord who spoke to her: "You are the God who sees me,"
for she said, "I have now seen the One who sees me." Gen 16:13

This was the beginning of God and I's journey to wooing me back into a place of pure trust and faith. Believing for the impossible and believing that God desires to bless me and give me the desires of my heart. To be more than just my Master and my Savior, but now to be my Husband. A soulmate with a heart for God.

As I sat there on the beach, God began to talk about this natural man that was going to be my new husband. He asked me so softly and tenderly, "What do you want in a husband?" I took a deep breath and said, "God I want a man that loves Wendy, the girl, knows my value and will be forever faithful to me. A man like you write about in *Gal*

5:22-26:

> "But the fruit of the spirit is love, joy, peace, forbearance, kindness, goodness, faithfulness, gentleness, and self-control. Against such things, there is no law. Those who belong to Christ Jesus have crucified the flesh with its passions and desires. Since we live by the Spirit, let us keep in step with the Spirit. Let us not become conceited, provoking and envying one another."

And in *Eph 5:25*:

> "Husbands, love your wives, just as Christ loved the church and gave himself up for her to make her holy, cleansing her by the washing with the water through the word."

Most importantly, he will allow me to be me, to laugh with me, dance with me, cry with me and do life and ministry with me. I heard God laugh and say, "Okay-okay, take a breath. Well, this man has the potential for all these, and his heart is good, but he is hard-headed. I need you to be patient as some of this will come in time, but all these characteristics exist in him. I want to give you a picture of him so that when you see him, you will know he is the one. Write this all down and keep it in your heart and mind:

- You will meet him in February.

- He is very tall

- He is Black, Tribe of Judah, like you. He showed me a flag of green, yellow, and red with a lion on it (I looked up later. It was the flag of Ethiopia)

- He is younger than you.

- He has matching tattoos on both arms (Huh? Tattoos really?). Then a picture popped in my head of an Egyptian eye

- He is very intelligent--that sometimes gets in his way. You will help him with this.

- He has a past, but he has a calling on his life. He's not yet a minister

- He needs his inheritance now. Study the Old Testament to help him with his lineage

- He has a daughter brand new, not a wife.

- Hollywood and New York are important to him. Be ready to go to both.

Here's the reason I chose you:

- He needs to know I love him enough to give him one of my most precious possessions, You.

- He needs affirmation. I will begin to fill you with so much love for him

- He will need the gift of tongues

- He will be sensitive to your health and eats a similar diet

- He is a truth seeker

"I need him, Wendy. I need you to impart wisdom, hope, faith, and revelation into him. You are capable of loving those with a past. He has one so just know I want to heal all of that. He has a Joseph anointing and is the baby in his family. His heart is like David."
"Wow, God, this is a lot. Thank you for choosing me, make me ready for all this. Protect my heart and bring him when he is ready."
God said, "Trust me, I got you. I am choosing Him because his heart is like yours. Before I put you both in your mothers' wombs, I let you meet each other. You will feel that soul connection when you meet him. He is your soulmate."

As God shared all this with me, I felt a tug on my heart. I felt a sense of honor that God chose me. My eyes filled with tears and my heart instantly felt whole again. I became so connected to God in the Spirit at that moment, all I could say is," Yes Lord, yes!, I trust you. Make me brave and ready to be his wife." I put the list in my bible and then took a much-needed walk on the beach.

As we were walking towards Starbucks, a white Maxima drives by super slow. I'm on automatic alert; I'm from Compton. Anyway, the car stops, the passenger window rolls down in slow motion. I hear a man's voice holler, "Wendy?"

What the??... I said, "YYYYes??" as I leaned down warily. The car then drove off to park. I whipped around and looked at my girlfriend. She had a huge sheepish grin on her face and said,

"Don't be mad, but I set you up."
"Oh no, you diunt!"

She went on my site and planned this date with this guy! I'm stuck meeting this guy. Lord, give me skrenff! Yes, I said, "skrenff."

Just as I'm about to let her have it, he walks up to us. I said, "Hi," in my nice little church girl voice. He hugged my girlfriend and then me. I gave him the Christian side-hug. We proceeded to get a table, and he asks if he can buy us coffee. We gave him the order, and he goes inside. I laid into my girlfriend, "This poor dude thinks I wanted this. Now what?" She says I got this just be your sweet self. "Girl, I'm about to cut you," I murmured. She laughed. Two minutes later he comes out and says," Um I just forgot everything you guys told me. Will one of you come with me?" My girlfriend says, "Wendy will." So, I got up and went inside with him. We were instantly handsy as if we've been long lost friends,

{Side note: Yes, he is great looking. Yes, he seems very nice, but I know nothing about this guy! I was so caught off guard; I started praying in tongues in my head. But my body is acting like, "Hey, what's your name, sexiness ☺". Lord help me. God gave me Is 42:6:

> *"I the Lord have called thee in righteousness, and will hold thine hand, and will keep thee, and give thee for a covenant of the people, for a light of the Gentiles..." Is 42-6*

I was like, "Really? God, what does that mean?" I hear God say, "Shhh, have peace." We get back outside, and my girlfriend begins drilling him with questions. "Are you single?" "Yes," he said confidently. "Do you do drugs?" "No, never." "Are you looking for a girlfriend or a wife?" "Yes." "Okay, last question, do you love God and are you a Christian?" He says, "Oh most definitely. Saved since I was 8-years old". She's satisfied, so she excuses herself from the table, and now it's just Eric and I. As Tony the Tiger would say, Grrreat!

All of a sudden, I felt the Holy Spirit on me. I'm looking at Eric. Our eyes lock, and something otherworldly just took over. I've never felt anything like this. I try making small talk, but he's not really responding. Then all of a sudden, he says, "You don't really look like your picture." I'm thinking, 'oh dear he's disappointed.' I guess my face told on me, because he says, "You're just way more beautiful in person." I said, "Thank you," and he reached his hand over to hold mine tightly. It was so amazing: the chemistry, the Holy Spirit, the peace of God that flooded me like a warm blanket around my shoulders. I heard God whisper, "I am right here." All of it felt like I was in a movie.

I couldn't really talk. His eyes were telling me so much. Then all of a sudden, he says, "Can I please just kiss you so I can focus." Huh? Okay. I haven't dated much, but is that really acceptable? I just met him. (That's what my head said) My body just leaned over and kissed him. Oh my God!, I felt a shock, a tingling on my lips. It was a wrap for me. I have no idea what he said after that. I was in-love.

Scripture Meditation: *Mal 3:10 (NIV)*:

> *"Bring the whole tithe into the storehouse, that there may be food in my house. Test me in this," says the* LORD *Almighty, "and see if I will not throw open the floodgates of heaven and pour out so much blessing that there will not be room enough to store it."*

Amen & Amen!!

Day 22: A 30-Day Bonus

Congratulations! You made it through twenty-one days of discovering God's infinite and extravagant love for you. Now the fun begins. Don't take this too lightly. It takes 63 days to create a habit. We're going to help you with the first 30.

Over the next 30 days, set a meeting time with Abba Father every morning and meditate on each of the ways listed below until these scriptures seep into you heart and you begin to increase intimacy with the Lover of our soul:

I will worship you and give you praise for I abide in you;

"He that dwells in the secret place of the most high shall abide in the shadow of the almighty," Ps 91:1

I will worship without compromise, Daniel 6:10-24:

Daniel in the Lions' Den

"Now when Daniel knew that the writing was signed, he went home. And in his upper room, with his windows open toward Jerusalem, he knelt down on his knees three times that day, and prayed and gave thanks before his God, as was his custom since early days. Then these men assembled and found Daniel praying and making supplication before his God. And they went before the king, and spoke concerning the king's decree: "Have you not signed a decree that every man who petitions any god or man within thirty days, except you, O king, shall be cast into the den of lions?" The king answered and said, "The thing is true, according to the law of the Medes and Persians, which does not alter." So they answered and said before the king, "That Daniel, who is one of the captives from Judah, does not show due regard for you, O king, or for the decree that you have signed, but makes his petition three times a day." And the king, when he heard these words, was greatly displeased with himself, and set his heart on Daniel to deliver him; and he labored till the going down of the sun to deliver him. Then these men approached the king, and said to the king, "Know, O king, that it is the law of the Medes and Persians that no decree or statute which the king establishes may be changed." So the king gave the command, and they brought Daniel and cast him into the den of lions. But the king spoke, saying to Daniel, "Your God, whom you serve continually, He will deliver you." Then a stone was brought and laid on the mouth of the den, and the king sealed it with his own signet ring and with the signets of his lords, that the purpose concerning Daniel might not be changed.

Daniel Saved from the Lions

Now the king went to his palace and spent the night fasting; and no musicians[b] were brought before him. Also his sleep went from him. Then the king arose very early in the morning and went in haste to the den of lions. And when he came to the den, he cried out with a lamenting voice to Daniel. The king spoke, saying to Daniel, "Daniel, servant of the living God, has your God, whom you serve continually, been able to deliver you from the lions?" Then Daniel said to the king, "O king, live forever! My God sent His angel and shut the lions' mouths, so that they have not hurt me, because I was found innocent before Him; and also, O king, I have done no wrong before you." Now the king was exceedingly glad for him, and commanded that they should take Daniel up out of the den. So Daniel was taken up out of the den, and no injury whatever was found on him, because he believed in his God.

Darius Honors God
And the king gave the command, and they brought those men who had accused Daniel, and they cast them into the den of lions—them, their children, and their wives; and the lions overpowered them, and broke all their bones in pieces before they ever came to the bottom of the den.

Lord I thank you that you fill my mouth with laughter:

Ps 126:2,3:
"Then our mouth was filled with laughter,
And our tongue with singing.
Then they said among the nations,
"The LORD has done great things for them."
The LORD has done great things for us,
And we are glad."

I will worship you before the rain:

"So Ahab went up to eat and drink. And Elijah went up to the top of Carmel; then he bowed down on the ground, and put his face between his knees, and said to his servant, "Go up now, look toward the sea." So he went up and looked, and said, "There is nothing." And seven times he said, "Go again." Then it came to pass the seventh time, that he said, "There is a cloud, as small as a man's hand, rising out of the sea!" So he said, "Go up, say to Ahab, 'Prepare your chariot, and go down before the rain stops you.'" Now it happened in the meantime that the sky became black with clouds and wind, and there was a heavy rain. So Ahab rode away and went to Jezreel.
1 King 18:42-45

Lord I will always remember that you are my first love:

"I know your works, your labor, your patience, and that you cannot bear those who are evil. And you have tested those who say they are apostles and are not, and have found them liars; and you have persevered and have patience, and have labored for My name's sake and have not become weary. Nevertheless I have this against you, that you

have left your first love." Rev 2:2-4

God you are perfect and faithful:

Lord, you are my God; I will exalt you and praise your name, for in perfect faithfulness you have done wonderful things, things planned long ago." Is 25:1 NIV

You are my God who blesses me and heals me:

"Worship the Lord your God, and his blessing will be on your food and water. I will take away sickness from among you." Ex 23:25

I will praise you always:
"Let everything that has breath praise the Lord." Ps 150:6 NIV

I will praise you in my trials:

"About midnight Paul and Silas were praying and singing hymns to God, and the other prisoners were listening to them." Acts 16:25 NIV

I worship you Holy Spirit:

"God is spirit, and his worshipers must worship in the Spirit and in truth." Jn 4:24 NIV

"I will praise you with not just my heart but with my soul: Praise the Lord, my soul; all my inmost being, praise his holy name." Ps 103:1 NIV

I praise you with a thankful heart for your love is everlasting:

Give thanks to the Lord, for he is good; his love endures forever." 1 Chr 16:34 NIV

I seek you Lord when I am thirsty:

"You, God, are my God, earnestly I seek you; I thirst for you, my whole being

longs for you, in a dry and parched land where there is no water." Ps 63:1 | NIV

I will praise you even when things look bare or in lack:

> *"Though the fig tree does not bud and there are no grapes on the vines, though the olive crop fails and the fields produce no food, though there are no sheep in the pen and no cattle in the stalls, yet I will rejoice in the Lord, I will be joyful in God my Savior." Hab 3:17-18 NIV*

I will praise you non-stop Lord:

> *"My mouth is filled with your praise, declaring your splendor all day long." Ps 71:8 | NIV*

I will praise you for being our comfort and compassion:

> *"Praise be to the God and Father of our Lord Jesus Christ, the Father of compassion and the God of all comfort, who comforts us in all our troubles, so that we can comfort those in any trouble with the comfort we ourselves receive from God." 2 Cor 1:3-4 NIV*

Epilogue

From: The Lord

To: Wendy Darline

Re: A Love Letter

(*This letter came from the Lord for such a time as this. God needs you to know this. Please let it speak directly to you and minister to your heart*)

(*Insert your name wherever you see mine*)

Dear _____,

I know everything about you. *Ps 139:1*
I know when you sit down and when you rise up. *Ps 139:2*
I am familiar with all your ways. *Ps 139:3*
For I knew you before I put you into your mother's womb. *Jer 1:45*
I made you in my likeness. *Gen 1:27*
You are fearfully and wonderfully made. *Ps 139:14*
I am not distant nor am I angry, but I am the complete expression of Love. *1 Jn 4:16*
It is my desire to lavish my love on you because I love you with an everlasting love.
1 Jn 3:1; Jer 31:3

My plan for your future has always been filled with hope. *Jer 29:11*
My thoughts toward you are countless as the sand on the seashores *Ps 139:17-18*
I rejoice over you with singing. *Zeph 3:17*
I will never stop doing good to you. *Jer 32:40*
You, Wendy Darline, are my treasured possession. *Ex 19:5*
I desire to establish you with all my heart and all my soul. *Jer 32:41*
I want to show you great and marvelous things. *Jer 33:3*
Delight yourself in me and I will give you the desires of your heart. *Ps 37:4*
Because I gave these desires to you. *Phil 2:13*
I am able to do more for you than you could possibly imagine. *Eph 3:20*
For I am your Great Encourager. *2Thes 2:16-17*
I am also your father who comforts you in all your troubles. *2 Cor 1:3-4*
When you are brokenhearted, I will be close to you. *Ps 34:18*
I will never leave you or forsake you. *Deut 31:6*
I will wipe away every tear from your eyes. *Rev 21:3-4*
I will take away all pain you have suffered here on this earth. *Rev 21:3-4*
Because I am your Father, and I love you even as I love my son Jesus. *Jn 17:23*
Jesus is my love for you revealed in the flesh. *Jn 17:26*
He came to show you that I am for you not against you. *Rom 8:31*
I tell you that I am not counting your sins. *2 Cor 5:18-19*
I gave up everything I loved so that I might gain your love. *Rom 8:31-32*
Nothing will ever separate you from my Love again. *Rom 8:38-39*
Come here to me, watch and see how I will vindicate you. *Rom 12:19*
I will give you rest. *Mt 11:28-29*
I will restore you. *Joel 2:25*
I will restore your health, and heal all your wounds. *Jer 30:17*
I have anointed you. *Lk 4:18; Is 61:1*
You are the splendor of Me, your King, strengthened with power through my spirit.
Eph 3:16-19
I created you to be a beautiful crown from among all the ash! *Is 61:3b*
Take this oil of gladness that I have made and prepare yourself to be a bride. *Is 61:3*

Love your Father,
God

"Therefore be imitators of God as dear children. And walk in love, as Christ also has loved us and given Himself for us, an offering and a sacrifice to God for a sweet-smelling aroma." Eph 5:1-2

Call To Salvation Prayer:

Lord God,
I want you in my life. I need to know you. I need a relationship with
you. Be my Lord. Be my savior. Forgive me for all of my sins. Thank
you for sending your only begotten son, Jesus Christ, to die on the
cross for me and resurrecting him. From this day forward, Jesus
Christ is the Lord of my life. Forever and ever. Amen.

Dedicate/Rededicate Your Heart to God
Prayer:

My Lord & God,
Thank you for hearing my prayers. Forgive me for not seeking you
diligently day in and day out. I have let the issues of the world
interrupt and steal our time together. I repent wholeheartedly for
putting anything before You. I choose from this moment forward to
make You the most important person in my life and to cherish our
time together. I will include You in all of my decision-making. I will
move when Your Spirit of Power comes upon me and not hesitate. I
believe in You. I want You and need You as the anchor in my life. I
pledge to give all praise, all glory, and all honor to You, The Most
High God, in every part of my life and being.
In Jesus' Name, Amen.

Prayer For Forgiveness:

Father God, I forgive all of those who have hurt me in any way. I
release them back to you so that I can receive your complete love for
me. I also forgive myself for the choses I made that went against
your heart and your Word. In Jesus' Name, Amen

Overcoming Depression/Oppression/Suicide Prayer:

Father God,
I come to you now asking for the Spirit of Love, Power, and a Sound Mind to come into my life. My hope is no longer deferred and my heart is forever protected by you. I thank you for your love and I plead the blood of Jesus over my mind. By your stripes I am healed in Jesus' Mighty Name. Amen (Read 2 Tim1:7)

Make sure you sign up for Eric & Wendy's Facebook group, 'The Prodigal Couples," to keep updated on their free giveaways, newest books, devotionals, in-store book signings, speaking engagements, seminars, marriage reconciliation boot camps and upcoming entertainment media productions.

If you loved reading *Extravagantly Loved,* don't forget to pick up Eric and Wendy's #1 Best Seller, *The Prodigal Couple*, on Amazon https://www.amazon.com/Prodigal-Couple-Extraordinary-Experienc e-Extravagant-ebook/dp/B076ZV6KYM/ref=sr_1_1?s=digital-text&ie =UTF8&qid=1529034692&sr=1-1&keywords=the+prodigal+couple

Coming Media Attractions:

I'm In Love
His Love Endures Forever
The Prodigal Couple Mens & Womens Devotional
The Prodigal Couple Prayer Book
The Prodigal Couple YouTube Channel

What Now?

* Join our social media family:

Facebook - @theingramsinternational
Twitter - @prodigalcouple
Instagram - #theprodigalcouple
Tumblr – theprodigalcouple

* Sign up for the prodigal couple website to keep updated with coming attractions, blogs, events, and merchandise at www.prodigalcouple.com

* Reread the book with your spouse/partner. Discuss your answers.

* Meditate on the scriptures in each chapter of this book. What is the Holy Spirit telling you to do about them?

* Reread your notes. Ask The Holy Spirit to reveal what vows you made or leftover bitterness or unforgiveness for experiences you endured that may be hardening your heart toward God.

Once the issues are revealed, immediately pray this:

Lord, thank you for revealing (issue/problem/lie of the enemy/vow). I ask that you pull up the root out of my heart and replace it with (find scriptures that say what God says about that issue), I.e., if bitterness is your issue, you would say,
"I
ask that you pull that root out of my heart and replace it with Hebrews 12:15:
"See
to it that no one fails to obtain the grace of God; that no "root of bitterness" springs
up and causes trouble, and by it many become defiled." In Jesus' Mighty Name, Amen.

* If any topic/subject in this book offended you, ask The Holy Spirit why it offended you? That may be the revealing of a root you need to pull up and get rid of so you can be healed in that area of your life.

* Have the talk about the issues that led the relationship astray

* Pray together in the morning, noon, and night about healing your relationship

* Start a 'Seeking God's Love study group with other couples

* Do some *spirit* cleaning! Rid your atmosphere of your old self and create new, God-filled memories!

* Journal all of the expressions of extravagant love that the Lord bestows on you and your relationship.

* Create a daily routine that starts with spending time with God and the desires on *His* heart.

* Before you leave for work in the morning and before you go to bed, speak 5 biblical compliments that express God's extravagant love for you and your spouse. (You can add more, but start with the Biblical ones to building up their spirit man/woman)

You were not created to be miserable and heartbroken.
You were not created to suffer through life.
You were created to love, worship, and be in a relationship with God.
Satan prowls around like a roaring lion seeking whose
love he can steal, kill, destroy and devour. Don't let it be yours.
Please join with us in praying daily for the healing of broken hearts,
depression, anger, bitterness and betrayal.
God loves You extravagantly.
Jesus loves you, His Bride, extravagantly.
Now it's time to for you to love God the way Jesus did.

Thank you for taking the time to read this book and allowing us to express how in love with God we are. We pray this book inspires you, heals you and sets you on a journey seeking God's love like never before, in Jesus' Mighty Name. Amen!

Wendy Darline and Eric Ingram
Co-Authors, Spirit-mates, Servants and Children of Almighty God

www.ingramcontent.com/pod-product-compliance
Lightning Source LLC
Chambersburg PA
CBHW031553040426
42452CB00006B/291

* 9 7 8 1 7 3 2 4 0 8 4 0 1 *